FAKE

NEWS

SEPARATING
TRUTH
FROM FICTION

MICHAEL MILLER

TF
CB

TWENTY-FIRST CENTURY BOOKS / MINNEAPOLIS

To my grandchildren—
Collin, Alethia, Hayley, Judah, Lael, and Jackson—
who have to navigate this new world of fake news.

Twenty-First Century Books
A division of Lerner Publishing Group, Inc.
241 First Avenue North
Minneapolis, MN 55401 USA

For reading levels and more information, look up this title at www.lernerbooks.com.

Main body text set in Adobe Garamond Pro 11/14
Typeface provided by Adobe.

Library of Congress Cataloging-in-Publication Data

Names: Miller, Michael, 1958– author.
Title: Fake news : separating truth from fiction / Michael Miller.
Description: Minneapolis : Twenty-First Century Books, 2018. | Includes bibliographical
    references and index. |
Identifiers: LCCN 2018010572 (print) | LCCN 2018012982 (ebook) |
    ISBN 9781541543928 (eb pdf) | ISBN 9781541528147 (lb : alk. paper)
Subjects: LCSH: Fake news. | Journalism—History—21st century.
Classification: LCC PN4784.F27 (ebook) | LCC PN4784.F27 M55 2018 (print) |
    DDC 070.4/3—dc23

LC record available at https://lccn.loc.gov/2018010572

Manufactured in the United States of America
1-44690-35529-7/6/2018

CONTENTS

CHAPTER 1
FAKE NEWS: IT'S REAL AND IT MATTERS

In 2016 more than a dozen candidates ran in the Republican Party primaries, state elections that helped determine the party's nominee for president of the United States. Among the top candidates were Donald Trump, a New York real estate developer and reality TV star, and Ted Cruz, a US senator from Texas.

Stretching over the first half of the year, the primary campaign grew increasingly nasty, with ugly name-calling and verbal insults. For example, on May 3, during an appearance on the Fox News television channel, Trump attacked Cruz's father, Rafael, a Cuban-born Christian preacher. Trump accused the elder Cruz of having associated with Lee Harvey Oswald. On November 22, 1963, Oswald assassinated John F. Kennedy, the nation's beloved young president, in Dallas, Texas. The assassination was shocking and sent Americans into deep mourning. Millions of Americans watched the funeral live on television.

"What was [Rafael Cruz] doing with Lee Harvey Oswald shortly before the death? Before the shooting?" Trump asked. "It's horrible."

Trump was referring to a story that had run in the *National Enquirer*, a tabloid newspaper, several weeks earlier. The headline read, "Ted Cruz's Father—Caught with JFK Assassin." The story claimed

Donald Trump referenced an untrue news story about the father of rival Republican candidate Ted Cruz (*right*) during the 2016 presidential primaries. After his election, Trump used the "fake news" label to discredit stories that criticized him.

that the elder Cruz had worked with Oswald three months before the assassination, and it included a photograph of Oswald with a man whom the newspaper identified as Rafael Cruz.

Even though the *National Enquirer* is well known for publishing false stories, many Americans believed the article. Countless numbers shared it on Facebook, Twitter, and other social media. It likely convinced some Republican primary voters not to cast a ballot for Cruz. Yet the story was fictional. It was fake news.

What Is Fake News?

People use the term *fake news* in two ways. First, it applies to news stories and social media posts posing, falsely, as genuine news items. These stories and posts are demonstrably untrue and deliberately designed to mislead the reader or viewer. The "fake news" label is also used to cast doubt on legitimate news stories, especially those that portray persons of power or celebrity in a negative light.

Why create fake news? Some people do it for money. They operate websites supported by online advertisements. The more visitors the websites receive, the more money the sites earn from advertisers. So the sites tempt readers to click on stories about shocking crimes, medical procedures gone wrong, and other sensational topics. Some headlines, such as "Cannibals Arrested in Florida Claim Eating Human Flesh Cures Diabetes and Depression," are over-the-top outrageous. But site operators have found that the more outrageous the headline, the more likely it is to attract clicks—even by people who know the story is likely untrue.

Others create fake news stories with the intent of influencing voters. For instance, during the 2016 US presidential election, many fake news articles contained outrageous falsehoods about the Democratic candidate, former secretary of state Hillary Clinton. Hoping to convince voters that Clinton was linked to sinister deals, a site claiming to be a Denver, Colorado, news organization ran a false article titled "FBI Agent Suspected in Hillary Email Leaks Found Dead in Apartment Murder-Suicide." The goal of such fake news is to sway opinions, either driving potential voters away from a candidate or encouraging votes for that candidate's opponent.

Many politically based fake news articles might sound as if they could be true, but when examined closely, they are deceptive at best or damagingly false at worst. Still, many people believe them. Why? Some fake news stories reinforce already existing beliefs. If some people already believed falsely that former US president Barack Obama is a Muslim, they might not question the fake news headline "NYC Muslim Terrorist Donated Thousands to Barack Obama's Campaigns." Others believe fabricated (made-up) stories simply because they see them in a news feed. The stories look "official," so readers don't question them. Or they might believe a story because they trust the friend who posted it.

Typically and historically, political forces on the right (conservative) side of the political spectrum rather than on the left (liberal) side generate and spread fake news and claims of fake news more often. "On Facebook, extreme hard right pages . . . share the widest range of known junk news sources and circulate more junk news than all the other audiences put together," wrote technology researchers from Oxford University in Britain in 2018. Psychologists say that people with conservative leanings tend to be warier of danger and potential threats, such as threats of crime or terrorism, than are liberals. And since many fake news stories tell of secret plots, crimes, and other frightening events, they are more likely to capture the attention of conservatives than of liberals. "Conservatives approach the situation from the start with greater [reaction] to threat, a greater prior belief [as] to the level of danger in the world, so it is logical for the conservative to take more seriously information about hazards than the liberal does," explains Daniel Fessler, a professor of anthropology at the University of California–Los Angeles.

What Fake News Isn't

The tactic of claiming that a legitimate news story is fake is typically used by politicians and other public figures to dismiss real news stories that present them in a negative light. Donald Trump, who won the US presidential election in 2016, often charges that stories that accurately accuse him or his associates of wrongdoing are "fake news." But he isn't alone. A number of other US politicians have adopted this technique. Paul LePage, the governor of Maine, dismissed a 2017 story about him considering a run for the US Senate as "fake news." LePage's beef with the story was that it did not adequately praise his accomplishments as governor and that it included quotes from a liberal political science professor. Brooke Ashjian, president of the school board in Fresno, California, accused a local reporter of writing fake news in a series of critical newspaper articles about high rates of teen pregnancy in Fresno.

POLITICAL LABELS

In the political arena, fake news comes out of different ideological camps. The terms *conservative and right wing* describe politicians and others who tend to hold traditional views about marriage, religion, family, gender, and patriotism. They generally want to see smaller government with fewer social programs and less overall spending. They usually believe that the ideal family consists of a married heterosexual couple and their children. The terms *liberal, progressive*, and *left wing* refer to those who tend to have flexible views about marriage, family, religion, and other social norms. This group tends to support larger governments that offer a range of social programs and are willing to spend money to support them. In the twenty-first-century United States, most Republicans represent a conservative view, while most Democrats represent a liberal one. And within each party are differences of opinion, with some members holding more extreme views.

The reality is that many news items painted as "fake" by persons of power aren't fake at all. Even the most powerful people in the world can't make a genuine news story fake just by saying so. Just because you don't like something doesn't mean it's fake. You may not like rainy weather, but your opinion doesn't stop it from raining. Opinions are not facts.

Facts do not become less true just because someone doesn't like them. Yet dubbing a legitimate story "fake" can be a very effective political tool, especially if done repeatedly over time. A public figure who doesn't like a particular news story that is truthful may smear the story as "fake news" and the source as part of the "fake news media." The repeated use of the label "fake news" can cast doubt on the truthfulness of a story, the motives of the news organization that produced it, and the truthfulness of other stories produced by the same organization.

The Power of Fake News

Some fake news stories experience a sudden rise in the public consciousness, get a spike of attention, and then fade quickly. Other fake news stories have longer legs, bubbling around social media, television, and talk radio for weeks, months, or even years.

Take, for example, the story of Barack Obama's birth certificate. Prior to Obama's election to his first term as US president, in 2008, some of his opponents began circulating fake news stories claiming that Obama had been born in Kenya (the birthplace of his father). Had this been true, Obama would not have been eligible, according to the US Constitution, to be president of the United States. So-called birthers asked for the release of Obama's birth certificate to prove his US citizenship. They were so insistent—and the story gained such traction—that Obama finally did release his birth certificate. The State of Hawaii, where he was born, issued the document. Still convinced that Obama was not a US citizen, the birthers switched to the claim that the Hawaiian birth certificate was a forgery. By then the falsehood that Obama was not a US citizen had circulated widely. When Obama was up for reelection in 2012, as many as half of all Republican primary voters believed it.

Fake news doesn't just impact the political arena. Since the late 1990s, many parents have shared false medical stories. One major false claim is that vaccinations—received by children to prevent common childhood illnesses such as measles, mumps, and chickenpox—cause autism. This disorder first appears in children younger than two and persists throughout life. It can include a wide range of symptoms. Some people with autism have difficulty socializing and communicating. Others focus on only one area of interest, such as animals or trains. Others make repetitive movements, such as rocking back and forth. Most people with autism exhibit a combination of symptoms. The fake news that vaccines cause autism began with a fraudulent study by Dr. Andrew Wakefield published in a British medical journal in 1998.

Even after the study was discredited, headlines such as "Now It's Official: FDA [Food and Drug Administration] Announced That Vaccines Are Causing Autism!" continued to circulate online. Some actors, powerful politicians, and committed activists also falsely claimed that vaccines can cause autism. Believing the false stories, many American parents have refused to have their children vaccinated for whooping cough, measles, diphtheria, and other infectious diseases. Vaccine refusal puts communities at high risk for disease outbreaks. In fact, disease outbreaks and even deaths of unvaccinated children have occurred. In 2014, for example, a measles outbreak began at Disneyland in Southern California. Because many California parents had not had their children vaccinated, the disease quickly spread. Soon measles infected more than 150 people in the United States, Canada, and Mexico.

Fake News Isn't New

Fake news didn't begin in the social media era of the twenty-first century. People and organizations have been spreading lies, rumors, and false allegations for thousands of years. One of the earliest known cases of fake news occurred in ancient Rome in the first century BCE. Octavian, a politician, wanted to take power from General Mark Antony, one of the rulers of Rome. Octavian obtained a false document claiming that Antony had shifted his allegiance from Rome to Egypt. Octavian read the document to the Roman Senate. Upon hearing this fake news, the Senate stripped Antony of his command and forced him to flee the country.

Fake news flourished in succeeding centuries, with the information spread by word of mouth. In Europe, the majority Christian population frequently persecuted the minority Jewish population. Some Christians spread rumors that Jews were killing Christian children and using their blood to make wine and bread for the Jewish holiday of Passover. One such incident occurred in the French city of Blois in 1171. Fueled by the false news of Jews killing Christian children, the authorities arrested thirty-three of the city's Jews and burned them at the stake. Similar situations occurred hundreds of times over several centuries, resulting in thousands of Jewish deaths.

News began to spread much more quickly after 1439, when German goldsmith Johannes Gutenberg invented a printing press with movable type. This invention led to the widespread printing and distribution of broadsides (large sheets of paper printed with song lyrics and other text), newspapers, and books in Europe and North America. Printed materials played a major role in disseminating new ideas and information. For instance, in the sixteenth century, German religious professor Martin Luther used printed pamphlets and other documents to criticize the Catholic Church, which led to the creation of the Protestant branch of Christianity. In North America during the eighteenth century, colonists used pamphlets and newspapers to criticize their rulers in Great Britain. This criticism inspired colonists to fight for their independence in the American Revolution (1775–1783).

Newspapers and other printed materials also disseminated fake news. To attract readers, many early newspapers exaggerated stories or printed entirely fabricated news. For example, in 1835 the *New York Sun*—previously known for its serious reporting—ran a series of wildly popular articles that turned out to be fake news. These articles detailed the supposed discovery of life on the moon by Sir John Herschel, a well-known British astronomer. According to the articles, Herschel used a telescope to view all kinds of exotic moon life, including unicorns and batlike winged humanoids.

> **To attract readers, many early newspapers exaggerated stories or printed entirely fabricated news.**

FAKE NEWS IN NAZI GERMANY

The use of fake news was a vital part of spreading violent anti-Semitism (hatred of Jews) in Germany before and during World War II (1939–1945). During the lead-up to the war, German dictator Adolf Hitler described news outlets that criticized his policies as the *Lügenpresse* (lying press).

Hitler's Nazi Party eventually seized control of German newspapers, radio stations, and newsreel companies (which produced short news-based films shown in movie theaters) and used them to spread its own fake news. Much of this "news" took the form of propaganda: information that purposely misleads people and that promotes a particular point of view based on biased or false ideas. Using state-run media, the Nazi Party charged that Communists (those who support state ownership of all businesses, factories, land, and other property) wanted to take over German government and businesses. The Nazis falsely blamed Communist agitators for a fire that destroyed the Reichstag (the building that hosts the lower house of the German legislature). Hitler then had Communist lawmakers arrested, which left the Nazis with a majority of seats in the legislature. The legislature then passed the Enabling Act of 1933. The act allowed Hitler and his advisers to enact any laws they pleased, without the approval or involvement of lawmakers. Thus Hitler gained full dictatorial power.

The Nazi propaganda machine also spread hateful, false rumors about Germany's Jews. While Germany was suffering deep economic hardship, the propaganda accused Jews of stealing jobs and unfairly controlling banks and other financial institutions. It also described Jews as less morally fit than Christians in Germany. Over time, Nazi propaganda was able to dehumanize Jews, portraying them as figures of evil and weakening resistance to laws that discriminated against Jews. The Nazis enacted more than four hundred

Es lebe Deutschland!

This propaganda poster from around 1935 shows Adolf Hitler triumphantly holding the Nazi flag, with a multitude of supporters hailing him in the background. The German words at the bottom mean "Long live Germany."

decrees and regulations regarding German Jews, including those that barred Jews from German schools and universities, prohibited them from holding jobs with the German government, and restricted their work in medical, legal, financial, and other professions. Hitler's anti-Jewish efforts brought about the Holocaust. In this state-sponsored program, the Nazi government imprisoned and murdered more than six million Jews and other "undesirables" (including homosexuals, prisoners of war, non-Jewish religious minorities, Communists, and the physically and mentally disabled) before and during the war.

The stories were fiction, but they enticed many New Yorkers to buy the newspaper.

Questionable media spreading questionable stories continues in the modern era. In the United States and abroad, tabloids such as the *National Enquirer* and the *Weekly World News* manufacture many tantalizing stories out of thin air. From 1979 until the paper folded in 2007, the *Weekly World News* published a series of sensational and popular stories about the fictional Bat Boy, a half-human, half-bat creature who a team of government agents supposedly hunted across the country.

Why You Should Care about Fake News

Fake news—both made-up stories and charges that real news is actually false—can be damaging to individuals and to society. For example, one fake news report says you can cure diabetes by eating large quantities of carrots. While ingesting lots of carrots won't harm you, other than possibly turning your skin yellow or orange, if you also quit taking your normal diabetes medications because of this report, your diabetes will get worse. So believing this fake news could kill you.

It's also dangerous to believe that legitimate news is false just because a public figure calls it so. If you take all claims of fake news at face value, you may start disbelieving everything you read in the national newspapers or hear on TV news shows, even though the vast majority of that news is true. It has been accurately reported and fact-checked by news organization staff before publication.

Democratic societies rely on the press to report truthful information and to verify that politicians, business leaders, and other powerful people are acting lawfully and speaking truthfully. The founders of the United States believed that a free press was so important to democracy that it deserved specific constitutional protection. The First Amendment to the Constitution ensures that "Congress will make no law . . . abridging the freedom of speech, or of the press." So the US press is free of governmental oversight, censorship, and control and, in most cases, is free to criticize the government, without fear of punishment.

Experts believe that a free press is essential in ensuring that elected officials remain accountable to voters. And voters need accurate information to make wise decisions about whom they elect. The press

WORD ORIGINS: FAKE NEWS

The term *fake news* has been around since at least 1890. A headline from that year in the *Cincinnati Commercial Tribune* declared, "Secretary Brunnell Declares Fake News about His People Is Being Telegraphed over the Country." Also in 1890, the *Kearney (NE) Daily Hub* mentioned a "fake news" report in another newspaper.

Although the term remained in circulation, the first time many modern Americans heard it was at a January 11, 2017, news conference with president-elect Donald Trump. CNN had just issued a news report charging that Trump's campaign had worked secretly with the Russian government to ensure Trump's presidential victory. When asked about CNN's report, Trump responded, "It's all fake news. It's phony stuff. It didn't happen." The Russia story is still under investigation, and the term *fake news* has since become part of everyday language.

Fake news so dominated public discourse in 2017 that the American Dialect Society, which studies the English language in North America, named it the 2017 Word of the Year. (Technically, it's a phrase, not one word.) The United Kingdom's *Collins English Dictionary* also named it the Word of the Year. The American Dialect Society defines the term in two ways, as "disinformation or falsehoods presented as real news" and "actual news that is claimed to be untrue."

informs the electorate about candidates and those already serving in office and contributes to the functioning of a democratic government. Many scholars refer to the free press as the fourth estate—a term that has its roots in European tradition. Starting in the Middle Ages, European society was divided into three estates, or classes: the clergy, the nobility, and the commoners. Eighteenth-century British writers and politicians believed that the press was so important that it constituted a fourth estate. In modern times, the press is a key part of society that influences community life and holds people in power accountable to accepted standards of freedom and justice. Fake news and smearing real news as "fake" can undermine this important function and weaken institutions by causing citizens routinely to distrust what they read and see in the media and in public life.

Because fake news is so pervasive, we need to learn how to determine which news is real and which is fake. Not everything on TV, in the newspapers, or online is true. And not everything that someone we admire determines is "fake" is fake. Some information claiming to be true is false, and some information said to be false is true. For the survival of democratic societies, members must be able to tell the difference.

CHAPTER 2
HOW REAL NEWS WORKS

How do legitimate newspapers, radio, television, and online news sources produce their stories? Who ensures that a story is accurate? What do these news organizations do when a story is inaccurate? The processes and procedures used by legitimate news organizations—such as the *New York Times*, the *National Review*, CNN, and the Associated Press—explain why we can trust these organizations to deliver fair and truthful reporting. These procedures also differentiate legitimate news organizations from those that concoct fake news stories.

Traditional Journalism

Depending on its size, a legitimate news organization employs dozens if not hundreds of reporters, photographers, producers, and editors. The editors choose what stories to cover, and they send the reporters into the community to collect information. A reporter might work on a story for a few hours, a few days, several weeks, or even years, depending on the depth of the coverage desired and the complexity of the topic. For example, a story on a common traffic accident or a house fire might occupy only a few hours or less of a reporter's time, while

Reporters question Pennsylvania Democrat Conor Lamb, who won a seat in the US House of Representatives in 2018. In addition to interviewing individuals, journalists gather facts by searching through legal documents, business archives, and other written materials to put together a news story.

an investigation into a complicated political scandal or an ongoing war would require weeks, months, or years of ongoing investigation from multiple reporters.

A reporter observes, researches, and inquires. A reporter looks at circumstances and surroundings, such as the scene of a house fire. Who is on the scene? Are they frightened, angry, or worried? Research often requires digging into written records, such as legal documents, business archives, and police reports. It might involve reading books and articles by experts. A reporter will find information about names and dates and official accounts and analyses of a trial, crime, or other event. A reporter will interview people for the story, such as the next-door neighbor of a burglary suspect, a police officer working a case, the spokesperson from a company or organization connected to the story, or a scholar who specializes in the topic. The reporter uses the interviews, official documents, observations, and other facts to write a story.

After the journalist writes a draft of the article, staff at the news organization fact-check the story. This varies by organization. Some small news organizations can't afford to pay independent fact-checkers so they rely on journalists to do their own verification of facts. But most large national newspapers and magazines employ people to double-check every fact in a story. The fact-checker uses archives, databases, reference books, and government documents to verify that all the dates, statistics, and other data in the story are correct. The fact-checker may also talk to experts, consult earlier news stories about the topic, and talk to people who were interviewed for the story. Fact-checkers flag statements that might be misleading, imprecise, or inaccurate. The reporter then reviews and corrects them.

After the editor approves the story, a copy editor checks and corrects grammar, spelling, punctuation, and journalistic style. Most news organizations rely on specific dictionaries and established style guides to ensure consistency. Then the story is published, posted online, or read on the air over TV or radio.

Journalistic Integrity

The press takes its duty to inform the public seriously. Legitimate news organizations embrace journalistic integrity—a set of practices and procedures that ensure the accuracy and effectiveness of their reporting. For example, the Society of Professional Journalists (SPJ), an Indiana-based organization that promotes freedom of the press, publishes a Code of Ethics for its members. The introduction to this code states its purpose:

> Members of the Society of Professional Journalists believe that public enlightenment is the forerunner of justice and the foundation of democracy. Ethical journalism

strives to ensure the free exchange of information that
is accurate, fair and thorough. An ethical journalist acts
with integrity.

The codes direct journalists to

- seek truth and report it accurately and clearly
- minimize harm by treating sources, subjects of
  stories, and members of the public with respect and
  with regard for their safety and privacy
- act independently, without taking direction from
  government or business and without taking gifts,
  favors, or other enticements that could result in
  biased reporting
- be accountable and transparent—to explain
  journalistic decisions to the public, to acknowledge
  and correct mistakes in reporting, and to expose
  any unethical journalism within the organization

Most legitimate journalists and news gathering organizations follow
these or similar guidelines.

Recognizing and Correcting Mistakes

Accuracy and accountability are key to any journalistic set of ethics.
But no matter how diligent the staff of a news organization may be
in checking the facts of a story, mistakes sometimes make it into
print or into a broadcast or website. The methods a legitimate news
organization uses to handle mistakes separate trustworthy from
untrustworthy journalism.

If a story contains a simple error in reporting—such as an incorrect
date or a misspelling—most legitimate newspapers and news websites
will publish a correction as soon as they become aware of it. Media

organizations also typically have a public way for readers, viewers, and listeners to contribute opinions and corrections, through letters to the editor. People can mail in their letters, email or tweet them, or phone them in. Because of the volume of letters, a news organization can't always respond to every one. News staff will review them all and choose those that are most important to respond to or share with the public.

Most legitimate news organizations also have an editor or other staff member as a link between the news organization and the public. Often holding the title of ombudsman, public editor, or public advocate, this person is responsible for addressing any mistakes in the organization's coverage of a story. This includes everything from unclear wording to biased or discriminatory reporting to factual errors and perceptions of unfair reporting. If readers or viewers have questions or complaints, they can contact the ombudsman, who might respond to the concerns through a column in a newspaper or website or through a short audio or video piece on the air.

News organizations that regularly and respectfully acknowledge and correct mistakes and address questions from the public are typically legitimate, reliable news sources. You won't find an ombudsman working for an organization that concocts fictitious news stories. By definition, an ombudsman's role is to protect truth, so that person would not work for an organization that lacks concern for the truth, accuracy, and honest reporting.

Anonymous Sources

Reporters report the news, typically by interviewing sources. But not all sources are comfortable with speaking on the record, or having their names linked to the information they provide. For instance, an employee who tells a reporter about alleged wrongdoing at a business or government office might be fired if identified as the source of the accusations. So the employee might agree to speak only if the employee's name does not appear in the story.

AN HONEST MISTAKE

We all make mistakes. We transpose numbers by accident. We misremember something. Journalists are human and sometimes make unintentional errors in their newspaper or television reporting. A mistake in a story doesn't make the story fake. It makes it inaccurate. It's how the news organization handles that mistake that matters.

For example, in December 2017, CNN reported a story about Wikileaks (an organization that legally and illegally obtains government secrets and other confidential information and makes them public). The story claimed that during the 2016 presidential campaign, Wikileaks had offered the Trump presidential campaign private access to hacked Democratic National Committee emails before they were published on the internet. If the story were true, it would mean that the Trump campaign had illegally conspired with Wikileaks to sabotage Democratic candidates.

However, the story proved to be untrue. CNN's source had provided the wrong date for the conversation about the emails between Wikileaks and the Trump campaign. CNN reported that the date was September 4, 2016, when the actual date was September 14—a day after the emails were published. It was a simple one-digit error, and the incorrect date completely changed CNN's analysis of the situation.

The journalist quickly realized the error. According to journalistic standards, CNN issued this correction by tweet the day after the report:

> CNN's initial reporting of the date on an email sent to members of the
> Trump campaign about Wikileaks documents, which was confirmed
> by two sources to CNN, was incorrect. We have updated our story to
> include the correct date, and present the proper context for the timing
> of email.

President Trump chastised CNN for reporting "fake news." But it wasn't fake. It was a mistake. The key difference between the two—fake news and error—is that CNN admitted the mistake and corrected the original story, according to the accepted standards of ethical journalism.

Then reporters have two options. First, they can use the interview as "off the record" or "deep background" material. Then the reporter cannot include the information in a story. But the reporter can use the information as a jumping-off point for more research and interviews.

The other option is to treat the interviewee as an anonymous source. This means that the reporter can print, post, or broadcast information supplied by the interviewee, including direct quotes, but cannot give the interviewee's name. The reporter might refer to the interviewee as "an anonymous source," "a senior official," "a person familiar with the situation," "a key figure," or something similar. In most cases, reporters are not obligated to reveal the name of anonymous sources. "Shield laws," which vary by state, offer them some protection from being forced by a court to disclose their sources. Since anonymous sources are often key to exposing stories of wrongdoing and corruption, being able to use them is one of the main principles of freedom of the press.

Nevertheless, anonymous sources present challenges for legitimate news organizations. For example, a fact-checker often can't verify information provided by an anonymous source, since the fact-checker cannot contact that person. However, the facts from that source might be able to be confirmed another way.

Some critics charge that information from anonymous sources is fake news. But just because a source is anonymous does not mean that person is lying. Nor does it mean that the story is made up. Journalists have relied on anonymous sources for decades, and it has become increasingly common. Often those sources provide important, accurate information and tips that lead to stunning stories.

That doesn't mean that reporters, readers, and listeners should automatically trust information coming from anonymous sources. Sometimes sources want to be anonymous for devious reasons. For instance, some politicians might want to smear a political rival without having their name attached to the attack. Sometimes anonymous sources are simply mistaken. When a story links quotes or information to an unnamed source, readers and listeners can analyze the reliability of the story a number of ways. For example, if an anonymous source's information is extremely different from that of other stories, it might be false. The same is true if the information can't be verified through other sources. But if other, on-the-record sources are saying something similar, then the information is likely true. News consumers should also consider the history and reputation of the news organization and the reporter. If the newspaper, TV channel, or website is generally reliable and has won prestigious journalistic awards, then the anonymous sources are most likely trustworthy.

Nontraditional Journalism

Many reporters study journalism or communications in college. When they graduate with degrees in those fields, they often take jobs with major news organizations. But the internet has also opened the field of journalism to just about anyone who wants to participate online, even those without a formal degree. You don't need the backing of a big news organization to write a blog entry, post a tweet or YouTube video, or add something to a Facebook timeline. It's easy to do with only a personal computer or handheld device and an internet connection. So almost anyone with access to the right equipment can be listed as a reporter and post stories online.

Many internet journalists (called also nontraditional journalists or citizen journalists) operate with the utmost integrity. But others are biased and do not follow journalistic standards for fair and accurate reporting. They often don't work with editors and fact-checkers the way traditional journalists do, so no one is double-checking their reporting for accuracy, clarity, and objectivity.

Nontraditional journalism has some positives. A citizen journalist might tweet news stories as they break rather than running them through editors and fact-checkers before publication or broadcast.

DEEP THROAT

One of the most famous anonymous sources in US journalistic history was nicknamed Deep Throat. Under deep cover, Deep Throat provided essential behind-the-scenes information to *Washington Post* reporters Bob Woodward and Carl Bernstein in the early 1970s. Woodward and Bernstein were investigating the Watergate scandal, the June 1972 break-in at Democratic National Committee headquarters at the Watergate office complex in Washington, DC.

The break-in was part of a secret reelection campaign tied to Republican president Richard Nixon and carried out by Republican operatives. The goal was to spy on, lie about, and smear the reputations of Democratic candidates to help Nixon win reelection that fall. Nixon did win, but the ongoing scandal—with incriminating coverage from Woodward and Bernstein, much of it based on leads from Deep Throat—eventually led to his resignation from office in August 1974.

As part of their agreement with Deep Throat, Woodward and Bernstein promised not to reveal his identity. They kept their promise for more than thirty years. Then, in 2005, retired associate Federal Bureau of Investigation director Mark Felt told *Vanity Fair* magazine that he was Deep Throat. He spoke to Woodward and Bernstein under deep cover because he would have lost his job at the FBI if his name had been revealed publicly.

In 1973 *Washington Post* reporters Bob Woodward (*left*) and Carl Bernstein received the Pulitzer Prize for distinguished public service in journalism for reporting on the Watergate scandal.

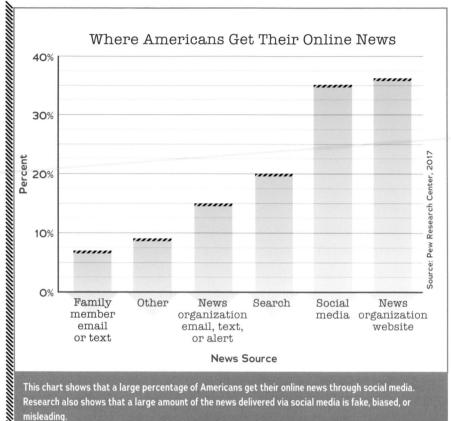

Where Americans Get Their Online News

Percent

- 40%
- 30%
- 20%
- 10%
- 0%

News Source:
- Family member email or text
- Other
- News organization email, text, or alert
- Search
- Social media
- News organization website

News Source

Source: Pew Research Center, 2017

This chart shows that a large percentage of Americans get their online news through social media. Research also shows that a large amount of the news delivered via social media is fake, biased, or misleading.

In the internet era, news consumers often value speed over precision. But a story reported quickly by a citizen journalist may not be as accurate or as in depth as the same story reported later in more depth by a larger or more traditional news outlet.

Media Bias

Bias is a preconceived preference for one viewpoint or another. In the world of media, bias is reporting that subtly or more obviously leans in a particular political direction, either right or left. Bias influences what stories a media organization covers and how they're covered.

While most legitimate news organizations try to maintain a nonbiased viewpoint, not all do. Some openly and purposely represent a specific point of view or philosophy through factual, well-researched, and well-reasoned reporting. For example, the *National Review* is a prominent US publication that reports news and opinions from a conservative standpoint. Reputable journalists write the articles and opinion pieces, and the magazine's print and online formats are well respected. On the other end of the political spectrum are journals such as *Mother Jones* and the *Nation*, both respected publications with an obvious liberal slant.

The stories right-leaning and left-leaning publications cover may be the same, but the conclusions they reach often differ dramatically. For example, one organization may paint a president's first year in office as a success, while another will describe it as a failure, with each source focusing on different facts and political philosophies to come to its conclusions. Reporters may point to a strong economy, job creation, and a strong stock market as evidence of the president's successes. Others will focus on turnover among the president's closest advisers, a rise in hate crimes, and accusations of wrongdoing by members of the administration as evidence of the president's failures. Media bias can result in stories receiving more or less attention than warranted, but if the news source holds to established journalistic standards, media bias does not necessarily result in false reporting.

Some news organizations—especially within the realm of cable TV news and online—go to extremes in presenting political biases. Their commentators might cherry-pick quotes and data—selecting only those that support a specific argument while ignoring the rest—to support a viewpoint. Critics have attacked Fox News (on the right) and MSNBC (on the left) for obviously biased reporting. However, political bias does not necessarily equate with fake news. A reporter can slant coverage and quote experts who have a particular viewpoint. But if the reporter can back up the research, confirm the facts, and stick to accepted journalistic standards, the story is not fake news.

CHAPTER 3
THE MANY FACES OF FAKE NEWS

Fake news isn't just one thing. Many different types of false information circulate online and through traditional print and broadcast media. Some of this information, such as stories about Bat Boy, is blatantly false. Other information is biased more than fictitious. It might have some kernel of truth, but its goal is to mislead or influence readers to think or act in a specific way.

Deliberately Fake Stories

The most blatantly fake news consists of deliberately bogus stories and posts, designed to mislead the public. These fake stories are filled with lies and make-believe "facts" about a particular person or topic. They describe events that didn't happen, often posted on websites designed to look like traditional news websites. This type of "traditional" fake news is fiction masquerading as real news.

A US company called Disinfomedia, which ceased operations in 2017, owned several such fake news sites, including NationalReport. net, USAToday.co, and WashingtonPost.co. Disinfomedia deliberately chose addresses that resembled the real *USA Today* and *Washington Post* sites to confuse casual visitors. (Note the .co domains instead of the normal .com domains.) The company knew that many visitors would click on the links, thinking they were visiting a reputable site. The sites

Fakes news is not hard to find. Most supermarkets stock tabloids filled with fake news. They are often at checkout counters alongside reputable magazines with accurate and reliable reporting.

published false stories based on real national news. One story from 2014, with the headline "Texas Town Quarantined after Family of Five Tests Positive for the Ebola Virus," played on fears of the deadly Ebola virus. Although a few people in Texas had contracted Ebola, there was no citywide quarantining and the disease was quickly contained in the United States.

While some people run blatantly fake news sites to influence political discourse, others do it to make money. Fake news sites generate money the way most websites do—with online advertising. The site signs up to an online advertising program, such as Google's AdSense, which in turn matches advertisers with website content. An ad is placed on a web page, and when someone clicks on the ad, the advertiser pays Google AdSense a small fee—pennies or even fractions of pennies (pay-per-click advertising). Google takes a cut of this advertising fee and pays the rest to the host website. The more users who visit the web pages and click the ads, the more revenue the site generates.

False Promises

Another type of fake news is fake science. Fake science stories usually present far-fetched medical claims. These claims often accompany quotes from people said to be doctors or scientists but typically with no credentials listed. For example, an article might cite "well-known scientists" or "research from a leading medical institution" without actually naming the scientists or institution. The article or ad might include statistics without saying what organization originally gathered them.

Many popular fake science stories claim to offer a cure for cancer through some sort of natural treatment. Often the hosting website offers that treatment for sale. So website operators might benefit from such stories through advertising revenue and by selling bogus cures.

Other fake news sites promote bogus products and get-rich-quick schemes. An example is sites promising that you can earn forty dollars an hour working from home. Those who click on these sites eventually find that they are the ones expected to pay. For a fee of about a hundred dollars, the sites offer to train the job seeker to be a fund-raiser, a product distributor, or a marketer. But the training is actually worthless, and the sites are scams.

Opinions

The expression of personal opinion has a long history in journalism. During the early years of the United States, newspapers were often associated with particular political viewpoints. The owners used their papers as platforms to forward their own political views. For example, former US treasury secretary Alexander Hamilton founded the *New York Evening Post* in 1801, and its editors publicized the views of Hamilton's Federalist Party. Later, newspapers separated their straight journalism from the opinions by printing the views of publishers, columnists, and readers in clearly labeled editorial pages.

In the 1960s and 1970s, TV stations often put a senior reporter, editor, or newsroom manager on the air to give a four- or five-minute editorial (an expression of opinion) at the end of the nightly news and labeled it on-screen as an editorial. Because of these labels, a viewer could easily distinguish between editorial segments and hard news.

Most newspapers still include editorial and opinion pages, separate from their main reporting. But with other media, the distinction between opinion and hard news is often fuzzy. Turn on any talk radio station or cable news network or listen to any web-based podcast and you'll encounter a large number of "talking heads." These people discuss the news of the day, often by offering their opinions about it rather than reporting facts.

In the twenty-first century, news and opinion intermix in most major media outlets. Some cable news networks have few if any traditional reporters on staff. They rely instead on political pundits (scholars and other experts) to provide analysis and commentary.

Cable TV hosts don't just report the news. Many of them, including Rachel Maddow (*left*) on MSNBC and Sean Hannity (*right*) on Fox, offer their opinions about the news.

Many programs with full reporting staff also include commentary from pundits to help the audience make sense of complex stories. Many talk radio stations offer mostly political commentary, with the hard news only in three-minute segments at the top of the hour. And many radio news programs invite call-in commentary from listeners, the majority of whom express their personal opinions on the stories of the day. Most web-based news organizations, such as CNN.com and Slate, offer a mix of straight reporting and opinion. Often it's difficult to know where the news stops and the opinions begin.

According to established journalistic standards and traditions, sharing opinions over the airwaves, in print, or online is okay as long as it's clearly understood to be opinion. Yet without clear guidance, many viewers, listeners, and readers take these opinions as facts and falsely view the commentators as reporters. The information that commentators share may be interesting and may state known truths, but it generally includes the commentator's biases. It's not hard news. It's opinion.

Propaganda

Fake news has its roots in propaganda. Throughout modern history, governments and politicians have used propaganda to spread incomplete or out-of-context facts and blatant untruths. The goal is to promote a specific cause or to discredit political opponents.

During World War I (1914–1918), for example, the US government produced posters, films, and pamphlets to convince citizens to hate the German enemy, support the US military, and enlist in the US Army. One poster showed the Germany military as an apelike beast obsessed with assaulting American women. The poster showed the beast grasping a bloody club in one hand and a half-naked young woman in the other to inspire Americans to hate and fear Germans. The poster encouraged young men to enlist in the army.

The Cold War (1945–1991) was a period of intense political,

Governments use propaganda to stir up feelings against perceived enemies and to promote patriotism among citizens. This US poster from World War I demonized the German enemy as an apelike beast and encouraged young men to join the US military.

military, economic, scientific, and cultural rivalry between the democratic United States and the Communist Soviet Union (a nation based in modern-day Russia). During the early years of this rivalry after World War II, the Soviet Union backed Communist takeovers of many nations. The Soviet Union and the United States never went to war, but US leaders feared that Soviet spies were operating in the United States. To counter Soviet influence, the US government and media companies used films, posters, advertisements, and magazine articles to convince Americans that communism was evil. The US military published guides on how to spot Communists, and Hollywood movies told horror stories about communism. In a 1949 film called *The Red Menace* (Red was a nickname for communism and Communists), a US military veteran named Bill Jones innocently joins the US Communist Party. He likes the party's ideas about equality for all. But he soon realizes his mistake. He learns that party leaders will stop at nothing—even murder—to punish those who question Communist ideals. Later, Jones cuts his ties with the Communists and reembraces democratic ideals. This movie and others helped feed Americans' fear of communism.

Nations still use propaganda. For example, China has built a multibillion-dollar media empire to spread pro-China propaganda around the globe. Part of the media effort includes a twenty-four-hour international English-language news channel. This propaganda, overseen by the Chinese Communist Party, praises the Chinese government, its leader Xi Jinping, and life in Communist China. These messages come through print, TV, film, and social media.

RED SCARE

Cold War propaganda was supposed to protect the United States from communism, but that propaganda itself hurt many innocent Americans. As the Cold War heated up in the late 1940s, several Americans were charged with passing on US government and military secrets to Soviet spies. The government then began searching for secret Communists working as federal employees. It established "loyalty boards" and fired workers suspected of having Communist leanings.

In the early 1950s, US senator Joseph McCarthy, a Republican from Wisconsin, held a series of congressional hearings to root out Communists from the US government and from society. As anti-Communist fever spread, some government agencies and private businesses required workers to take loyalty oaths, disavowing any connections to communism and swearing allegiance to the United States. Some companies fired or blacklisted (refused to hire) suspected Communists. Thousands of people with left-leaning political opinions, including university professors, entertainers, journalists, and members of the clergy, came under suspicion. Many lost their jobs.

Conspiracy Theories

Sometimes the line between fake news, opinion, and propaganda gets blurred. Conspiracy theories can fall into any or all of these categories. Conspiracy theories are explanations for events that challenge the official understanding of those events. They might be based on political biases, fake news, or a deep distrust of government, science, big corporations, or other powerful entities.

Conspiracy theories usually suggest that a secret plot among powerful people or organizations is covering up the truth of what really happened. For example, some Americans believe that President Kennedy's assassination in 1963 was part of a nefarious plot by the US Central Intelligence Agency and the Mafia. Others believe that the government faked the 1969 moon landing in a movie studio. Still others are convinced that aircraft spread chemtrails (chemical trails) designed to sicken the population or somehow control their minds. Despite facts proving otherwise, conspiracy theories persist. But a lone gunman, Lee Harvey Oswald, shot Kennedy; astronauts Neil Armstrong and Buzz Aldrin really did land on the moon in 1969; and those line-shaped "chemtrails" are nothing more than water vapor from jet engines.

One conspiracy theory concerns climate change—the upward shift in temperatures that has led to global shifts in Earth's weather patterns. Burning fossil fuels (coal, oil, and natural gas) emits carbon dioxide and other heat-trapping gases into Earth's atmosphere. Some people believe that climate change—established as a fact in the late twentieth century and understood to be true by 97 percent of the world's scientists—is a hoax concocted by scientists and environmentalists. Climate change deniers doubt the truthfulness of global warming statistics and say that any changes in Earth's climate are natural, not human-made. Climate change deniers believe that scientists, the alternative energy industry, and others have conspired to promote the idea of climate change so they can benefit from consulting fees, the funding of scientific studies, and the sale of solar panels, wind turbines, and other equipment that generates power without using fossil fuels.

Other conspiracy theorists say that the US government planned the terrorist attacks of September 11, 2001 (9/11). On that day, nineteen hijackers flew passenger airplanes into the World Trade Center towers in New York City; the Pentagon (headquarters of the US military) near Washington, DC; and into a field in Pennsylvania after passengers tried to stop them from their mission. So-called 9/11 "truthers" do not believe the reported facts that Middle Eastern terrorists masterminded the attacks. They believe, instead, that the US government planned the attacks to stir up US anger against Middle Easterners and to gain public acceptance for a coming war in the Middle East.

Climate change is real, and the US government did not plan the 9/11 attacks, yet the conspiracy theories persist. And they spread easily and quickly through social media, where conspiracy theories find a natural home. Social media makes it easy for people to share ideas, fact-based or not. On these social media, it's easy to gain exposure and followers. Because like-minded people tend to follow one another online, supporters typically outnumber challengers on any given site—which can make it seem as if a conspiracy theory has widespread support.

Why do people believe conspiracy theories? For some, it's a way of trying to make sense out of chaotic or disturbing events. They feel it isn't logical that a lone gunman could slip through the cracks and shoot a president or that a handful of foreign terrorists could hijack and fly airliners into buildings. They think there must be more to the story. Buying into a conspiracy theory helps them make order out of chaos.

Conspiracy theories are typically easy to dismiss. Usually the official explanation for an event—the one endorsed by traditional journalists, scholars, and governments—is the truth. Nothing more is behind the scenes. Still, conspiracy theories persist and contribute to the glut of fake news swirling around the internet.

Humor

Some fake news is fake for the sake of humor. Many websites manufacture humorous stories in the name of entertainment. Numerous late-night television shows, such as *Saturday Night Live* and *The Daily Show*, produce humorous skits that mimic real news coverage. Occasionally, viewers mistake a site or skit for honest-to-goodness news.

THE WAR OF THE WORLDS

One of the most famous instances of fake news in the United States occurred on October 30, 1938. In this era, before television broadcasted to homes, Americans got much of their news and entertainment by listening to the radio. The night before Halloween, CBS aired a special episode of *The Mercury Theatre on the Air*. Orson Welles (later a film star and director) directed and narrated this radio drama series. For this episode, Welles dramatized *The War of the Worlds*, a science-fiction novel by British writer H. G. Wells. The drama sounded like a normal evening music program, with a number of news bulletins inserted between musical segments. Then the bulletins became more frequent, with the news announcer saying, in a realistic fashion, that Martians had invaded Earth.

While the announcer had stated at the start of the program that it was purely fictional, many listeners tuned in late or didn't pay attention to that warning. Welles's production was so realistic that many listeners believed Martians were actually invading. Thousands of people called the police. Others fled their homes. In some places, roads filled with panic-stricken citizens trying to evacuate before the Martians invaded their towns.

When the uproar ended, Welles and the network made a number of public apologies. *The War of the Worlds* broadcast proved that well-executed fake news could easily mislead a gullible public.

The *Onion* is one of the most popular satirical sites on the internet. (Satire is a literary work that holds up human vices and folly to ridicule or scorn.) Founded in 1988 as a satirical print newspaper, the *Onion* eventually transitioned to an online publication. It publishes humorous made-up stories that borrows from current news. Its headlines have included laugh-out-loud statements such as "Drugs Win Drug War" and "Study Finds Every Style of Parenting Produces Disturbed, Miserable Adults."

Most of what the *Onion* publishes is silly, and anyone paying close attention wouldn't take it seriously. But not everyone pays close attention, and sometimes satirical stories from the *Onion* and similar outlets get mistaken for genuine news stories. So not everybody gets the joke.

Even legitimate news organizations occasionally have been fooled. In 2010 the *Onion* published a satirical story with the headline "Frustrated Obama Sends Nation Rambling 75,000-Word E-Mail." The story said that President Obama was fed up with Congress and unhappy with how the nation was faring economically and militarily. Someone at Fox News took this fake story seriously and republished it on the Fox News website. Because of its right-wing bias, Fox was eager to circulate a negative story about Obama. And since they had read it on Fox News, some readers shared the story through social media. Others posted anti-Obama comments on Fox's site in response to the story. Fox eventually realized its mistake and took down the story, but not before demonstrating how fake news can even fool experienced journalists—and how quickly false stories can spread.

CHAPTER 4
REAL FAKES

Some news really is fake. Many websites spread fake news articles, hoaxes, and disinformation to influence public opinion or to obscure the truth. These sites deliberately set out to make readers believe they're reading real news articles. Staff at the sites write pieces that sound believable but are false, hoping to lure readers to click on links.

Fake News for Profit

Amateurs (nonprofessionals) create some fake news for the fun of it. But professionals produce much of the fake news on the web and social media. These individuals, organizations, and governments research and target specific audiences and topics to maximize the number of visitors to their sites.

Often it's all about money. Fake news sites typically earn money by selling advertising. The more people who visit the site and click on the ads, the more money the site makes. The site might only earn a fraction of a cent per click, but multiply that by hundreds of thousands or millions of clicks, and the money adds up fast. That's why fake website operators hope that their stories go viral, spreading quickly to many people, and generating many millions of clicks—and thousands or tens of thousands of advertising dollars.

During the 2016 US presidential election, BuzzFeed editor Craig Silverman and UK social media researcher Lawrence Alexander tracked

On their fake news website Liberty Writers News, Paris Wade (*left*) and Ben Goldman (*right*) churn out false stories with an anti-liberal, pro-right-wing slant.

more than one hundred fake news websites to a small and impoverished former factory town called Veles in the southeastern European nation of Macedonia. These websites were producing a large volume of pro-Donald Trump and anti-Hillary Clinton stories (in English). The stories were popular, attracting a significant number of visitors—the owner of one such site averaged more than one million page views a month. Some stories on these sites were factual but had a pro-Trump bias. Others were completely and deliberately false.

The operators of many of these sites were young males. In their teens and twenties, they were in high school and university. Living in a town with few economic opportunities, they were looking for ways to make money. So they decided to create ad-supported websites. They did not have personal biases for or against Donald Trump, nor did they even have an interest in US politics. They didn't care if Trump won or lost the election. But they quickly discovered that the pro-Trump stories brought in the most traffic and therefore the most revenue from Google ads.

Like other webmasters before them, the Macedonian fake news factory found that promoting and sharing stories on Facebook drove traffic to their revenue-generating websites. People viewing the (mostly fake) posts would share them with their Facebook friends. Others clicked through to the host website, which helped increase traffic and ultimately revenues—which were significant. One young webmaster named Boris made close to $16,000 from his two websites in the four months before the US election. Boris became a rich man in a nation where the average monthly salary is just $371.

> **Some people spread fake news to support a particular ideology or a candidate in an election.**

The young webmasters in Macedonia aren't the only people to spread fake news for profit. The late Paul Horner, who wrote fake articles for a number of websites, claimed to take home $10,000 a month from AdSense alone. Paris Wade and Ben Goldman, the webmasters behind the fake news site Liberty Writers News, generated up to $40,000 per month in advertising revenues during the 2016 US presidential election. They wrote under the pseudonyms Paris Swade and Danny Gold.

Los Angeles–based Jestin Coler was the brains behind Disinfomedia, the company that ran NationalReport.net, USAToday.co, and WashingtonPost.co. Known as the King of Fake News, he works for a software company and is a Democrat. Coler says that he got into the fake news business in 2013, when he started the National Report site to show how quickly and easily fake news can spread. He later launched about twenty-five more sites. Like the Macedonians, Coler and his staff of writers found that stories reflecting right-wing politics drew the most visitors. So that's what his sites focused on. While Coler doesn't share specifics, he admits that he and his staff of writers earned a lot of money. He alone brought in about $30,000 per month from ad revenue.

Coler's first site (National Report) did include a disclaimer indicating that the stories readers would find there were fiction. But most visitors never saw it, and the site soon was racking up more than one hundred million page views per year. Then, in 2015, Facebook started marking stories from National Report as hoaxes, and site traffic dropped. To compensate, Coler started the more legitimate-looking site Denver Guardian, which featured some truthful information about sports, weather, and other local concerns. Facebook accepted that site as legit, so Coler snuck the occasional fake news story into that site.

But Coler went too far on November 5, 2016—two days before the presidential election. His Denver Guardian site ran the headline "FBI Suspected in Hillary Email Leaks Found Dead in Apparent Murder-Suicide." This post blew up on Facebook, at one point generating one hundred shares per minute. Coler had tried to avoid media attention himself, working under the pseudonym Allen Montgomery. But National Public Radio tracked him down and exposed him publicly. Not wanting the negative publicity, Coler shut down all his sites except for National Report, which he turned into a more satirical site.

The 2016 US Presidential Campaign

Not all people who produce fake news are in it for the money. Some spread fake news to support a particular ideology (political philosophy) or a candidate in an election. An increasing number of Americans say that social media outlets are their main source of news. So the many fictitious stories that spread through Facebook, Twitter, and other social networking services can strongly influence political views—and election results.

US investigators believe that Russian president Vladimir Putin directed operatives to interfere with the 2016 US presidential election. His goals were to create discord among US voters and to cast doubt on the democratic system of government. Another key goal was to swing the election for Donald Trump, whose policies are generally more favorable to Russia than those of Democratic candidate Hillary Clinton.

The 2016 US presidential election was influenced by manipulation of social media. During the campaign season, various organizations and people used Facebook and other networking services to spread misinformation, propaganda, and other fake news. Human agents and computer robots, or bots, spread these stories across social media, sometimes using fake social media accounts. The majority of these fabrications were anti-Clinton and pro-Trump. One analysis counted 115 pro-Trump fake stories on Facebook in the three months leading up to the election. People shared these stories 30 million times. During that time, people shared just 41 pro-Clinton fake stories on Facebook 7.6 million times.

Investigators have found that the Russian government and its agents generated a significant number of these stories. The goal of the Russians was to swing the election away from Clinton and toward Trump. Political scientists think that the president of Russia, Vladimir Putin, wanted Trump to win because Trump's views are more pro-Russia than Clinton's are. If Trump were elected president, his policies would be more favorable to Russia. Putin also knew that by disrupting the US democratic process, the fake news stories could sway voter behavior. And many of the stories specifically targeted voters in Michigan, Wisconsin, and Pennsylvania—states where the contest was extremely close. Trump won an unexpectedly close election, and many experts believe Russia's disinformation campaign contributed to his victory.

After Trump took office in January 2017, several governmental entities—including the FBI, the Department of Homeland Security, and both houses of Congress—began looking into the alleged Russian involvement in the election. The Department of Justice (DOJ) assigned attorney and former FBI director Robert Mueller III as special counsel to investigate potential Russian interference. Mueller's investigation also looked into the possible connection between Trump's campaign and the Russian effort.

On February 16, 2018, Mueller charged thirteen Russian individuals and three Russian companies of criminally conspiring to interfere with the election. The charges allege that the Internet Research Agency, based in Saint Petersburg, Russia, was the hub of online efforts to turn American voters against Clinton and to persuade them to cast votes for Trump.

Mueller's investigation discovered that Russians posing as Americans had purchased space on US-based computer servers. They had opened social media accounts in the United States and posted political messages that attacked Hillary Clinton. Shared by both humans and bots controlled by the Russians, the posts started showing up in the news feeds of Americans, who read and shared the fake news with their own online friends.

The DOJ believes the Internet Research Agency operated with a monthly budget of close to $1.25 million to buy targeted social media advertising that shared primarily pro-Trump material with people likely to support Trump. Twitter had 3,814 Internet Research Agency–linked accounts, which posted 175,993 tweets between September 1 and November 15, 2016. Also on Twitter, almost fifty thousand Russian bots created or retweeted more than 1.4 million election-related tweets, primarily in favor of Trump, during the same time. Facebook found that Russian operatives had placed more than 3,517 ads during the 2016 presidential campaign season. Most of them focused on hot-button issues, such as race and religion, which were likely to divide the voting public even further.

> **Social media companies, search engines, and other organizations are looking for ways to ban fake posts to prevent foreign meddling in future elections.**

The creation and dissemination of fake news was just part of the Russian campaign. Russian operatives also hacked into the computer servers of the Democratic Party and leaked data to the press. Russians even secretly organized rallies for and against both candidates in an attempt to promote discord among potential voters.

The Russian suspects conducted what US deputy attorney general Rod J. Rosenstein has called "information warfare against the United States with the stated goal of spread[ing] distrust towards

"[Investigations] concluded with high confidence that the Russians ran an extensive information war campaign against my campaign, to influence voters in the election. They did it through paid advertising we think, they did it through false news sites, they did it through these thousand agents, they did it through machine learning [bots with artificial intelligence], which you know, kept spewing out this stuff over and over again."

—Hillary Clinton, 2017, about campaign meddling in 2016

the candidates and the [US] political system in general." The Russians tried to make their posts look as if Americans produced them. To do so, they set up an eighty-person team of graphics specialists, data analysts, and search engine optimization experts to create and circulate false information. (Search engine optimization involves configuring a web page so that it shows up at the top of web search results—important to getting fake news in front of the maximum number of users.)

The Russian government denies any official involvement in the election meddling, and Trump denies knowing anything about it. But others in the US government, as well as social media companies, search engines, and other organizations are looking for ways to ban fake posts to prevent foreign meddling in future elections. For example, in November 2016, Google banned several hundred fake news websites from its AdSense advertising network. The ban was part of an update to its existing policy that prohibits sites that mislead visitors with their content. This action makes it more difficult for fake news sites to place ads and generate advertising revenue. But fake news sites still have options. For example, they can still buy ads on the many non-Google advertising platforms.

Social Media and Fake News

A survey from the Pew Research Center found that two-thirds of Americans say they get at least some of their news from social media, with 20 percent often doing so. Since most of the posts on social media are unverified (just about anybody can sign up and post, even using fake names), many Americans are getting what they think is "news" from untrustworthy sources.

A 2018 study found that during the final weeks of the 2016 US presidential election, more than one-quarter of American adults visited a page on a pro-Trump or pro-Clinton fake news website. Heavy Facebook users were more likely than Twitter or Google users to visit fake news sites. They often found the sites through posts and advertisements on Facebook.

Creators of fake news have several ways of spreading their stories on Facebook. First, they can set up and use dozens or hundreds of phony accounts to post fake news stories. By then friending other users, the humans or bots behind these accounts expose those users to the fake posts through Facebook news feeds. As friends of the friends view these stories in their own news feeds, the stories spread virally to thousands of other users.

How widespread is sharing fake news through social media? A Pew Research Center survey revealed that almost one-quarter (23 percent) of Americans said they have shared a fake news story. Another 14 percent said they shared a story they knew was fake. Almost one-third (32 percent) of respondents said they often see completely made-up stories online, and 51 percent say they often see news that they view as inaccurate.

Without social media, fake news would spread more slowly and to fewer people. Before social media, fake news and rumors spread through email, fax, postal mail, TV, and newspapers—all of which are slower and less wide-reaching than social media. While you can still spread unverified (or unverifiable) information by email, your audience is likely to be limited to your immediate friends and family. Posting on social media widens your audience and lets it spread quickly via sharing and resharing. As Matthew Gentzkow, an economics professor at Stanford University, explained in 2017, "Social media have changed things by making it much easier to spread fake news. And it makes fake news financially profitable."

CHAPTER 5
WHO BELIEVES FAKE NEWS, AND WHY?

Fake news has its appeal to certain people. Some people are more attracted to fake news than they are to the real stuff. For example, a BuzzFeed analysis found that during the final three months of the 2016 presidential election, the twenty most popular fake news stories on Facebook generated 1.3 million more engagements (shares, likes, and so on) than did the twenty most popular real news stories on the site. Most of the fake stories were obviously fake. One of them claimed that Hillary Clinton had sold weapons to the terrorist Islamic state (ISIS). Yet many Facebook users shared and presumably believed them.

Why do people believe obviously false stories? Who's falling for all this fake information—and why?

People with a certain frame of mind and worldview are more prone than other people to believe certain types of information. And the places where they find this information matters too. Certain sources are more believable than other sources—at least to certain people.

We Trust Others Like Us

As a social species, human beings have a tendency to group other people into easily grasped categories. The categories may be race, religion, gender, sexual orientation, political party, or region. Putting people into categories can be helpful in understanding a complex world, but it also has the negative effect of creating and reinforcing stereotypes. And stereotypes can make it difficult to see people as individuals.

The attitudes that a person has about an entire group of people—such as a racial or religious group—are what psychologists call implicit bias. Implicit bias usually results in trusting members of your own group more than those of a different group. If you're a conservative Christian, for example, you might tend to trust other conservative Christians over more liberal Christians or people of another religion. You might develop a bias *against* those of the Jewish or Muslim or progressive Christian faiths because they're not in your specific group. It's the same if your politics are liberal. A person will tend to believe

Humanity is diverse. Psychologists point out that people tend to trust others like themselves and to distrust those in other ethnic, racial, or political groups. Those who create and spread fake news take advantage of this human tendency and use it to promote stereotypes and stir up hatred.

other liberals and dismiss views of conservatives. Implicit bias pits one group against another.

Implicit bias is shaped by experience, often from a very young age. It colors the way we view people and how we act toward them, often negatively. We may fear someone because of the color of that person's skin. Sometimes the effect is positive. For example, we might be drawn to people from a country we think is unique and exciting.

One of the dangers of implicit bias is that people often too easily believe people of their own group. They do not admit that they and their group might be wrong about an issue. Also, they are more likely to dismiss the views of people outside their group, even when those views are important or helpful. Implicit bias makes people more prone to believe fake news that comes from someone of the same group. It can also make people label real news as fake if that news comes from someone in a different group.

We Want Comfort and Certainty

Sometimes the truth is uncomfortable or scary. Sometimes the truth is complicated. Sometimes the truth isn't what we want to hear. Fake news often presents a more comfortable, positive, and easier-to-understand reality than real news. Fake news often tells us what we want to believe rather than what actually exists. It reinforces our prejudices and beliefs. It makes us feel better.

Consider the topic of climate change. Humans burn vast amounts of fossil fuels (coal, oil, and natural gas), which release heat-trapping carbon dioxide and other gases into the atmosphere. Because of the gases, Earth and its oceans are heating up. The warmer temperatures are changing weather patterns and leading to more powerful storms, droughts, and other weather extremes. Higher temperatures on Earth are also melting ice at the North Pole and South Pole. Sea levels are rising, leading to the flooding of islands and coastal cities. Climate change is also shifting animal and plant habitats. Sometimes plants and animals cannot adjust and are dying off. If humans hope to reverse the effects of climate change, we have to change our behavior—in big ways and small, and quickly. We have to burn far less fossil fuels and invest in alternative energy, such as wind and solar power. These changes are not easy to make, and often they are expensive to install. They may even threaten ways of doing business, growing crops, and traveling from one place to another that have been around for decades.

Numerous scientific studies have proven that climate change is scientific fact. It is not fake news. But it is bad news. And many people don't want to face it. They don't want to hear that Earth is heating up; that higher temperatures are threatening plant, animal, and human life; and that we need to change our behavior to halt the damage. It's more comforting to believe fake news stories that deny climate change. It's easier, for some, to believe that climate scientists are falsifying their studies so they can make money promoting the "climate change industry." For some, the fake stories are easier to accept than the real story.

The simplicity and certainty promised by fake news can be appealing. If you or someone you love has a life-threatening disease, you might desperately want to believe that a new pill or treatment by phone will provide a cure. If you're deeply in debt or can't find a job, you may want to believe that the latest work-from-home scheme really does pay forty dollars an hour. In a world filled with uncertainty and fear, people often fall for ideas that promise to make life better, safer, and more comfortable.

If It Seems Reasonable, We Believe It

Sometimes all it takes to get people to believe fake news is for that news to seem reasonable. What types of stories sound reasonable? It depends somewhat on what you already know. For example, you might know that the US National Aeronautics and Space Administration (NASA) is looking for signs of life on other planets. So if you read a news story claiming that NASA has found microbes on Mars, it might sound reasonable enough to be true (even though it isn't). But a story that claims that aliens are plotting to overthrow Earth from a secret moon base is too outlandish for most people to find believable.

We Believe What Confirms Our Biases

Believing in and spreading fake news is often related to whether disinformation plays into our preconceived notions of the truth. Fake news that confirms the biases and ideas we already have doesn't seem fake.

For example, if you are left-handed and find a story that claims that left-handed people are more intelligent than right-handed people, you might believe it—without checking out the claim. And you might be skeptical of a story that claims that left-handed people are less intelligent than right-handed people, even if that story contained verifiable facts backing up the claim.

Confirmation bias is the often conscious tendency to believe things that confirm our existing biases and beliefs. This type of bias leads people to accept things on face value without fact-checking what they read or hear. If you already believe that left-handed people are smarter than right-handers, for instance, then you think you don't need to double-check that story. Or you think you don't need to read about the research that backs up the reporter's claims. The story must be true, you think, because it confirms your belief.

But if you're a left-hander and you read a story saying that right-handers are smarter, you may dismiss that story as fake without double-checking it. The story *just can't be true*, your confirmation bias tells you, even if it cites reliable studies and data. You dismiss the story without checking it out because your confirmation bias tells you it's false.

Confirmation bias is a major factor in believing fake news stories or disbelieving factual stories that disagree with existing views. Because of confirmation bias, we believe what we want to believe, no matter what the facts say. Studies show that people will actively ignore information that contradicts their beliefs—or they will focus only on the parts of a story that reinforce their thinking.

We Trust Intuition over Fact

Some people rely heavily on facts. They don't like or trust hearsay and rumors. They need to see the facts that back up any statement. Other people are more likely to trust their intuition. They don't need, want, or look for a lot of facts to trust statements that strike them as believable.

For example, your intuition may tell you that genetically modified (GM) foods are unsafe. GM foods come from plants or animals whose genes (chemicals inside cells that determine an organism's traits) have been changed in a laboratory to create a new organism or a new feature of that organism. Scientists often genetically modify crops to make them more resistant to pests or disease. This results in more plentiful food harvests. GM foods can help in the fight against world hunger. But many people have a gut sense that tampering with food in a lab just can't be safe. They are more likely to believe websites and articles that call GM foods Frankenfoods. (This term comes from the Frankenstein monster, a character in an 1818 horror novel by British author Mary Shelley.) Most scientific organizations say that GM foods are safe, but many consumers trust their guts and avoid them.

Studies have shown that people who trust their guts over scientific data are more likely to believe fake news. One 2017 Ohio State University and the University of Michigan study asked participants about climate change, well-known conspiracy theories, and the unconfirmed link between vaccines and autism. The study revealed that people who agreed with the statement "I trust my gut to tell me what's true and what's not" were more likely to believe fake news and conspiracy theories. Those who agreed with the statement "Evidence is more important than whether something feels true" were less likely to believe such falsehoods. As study coauthor Brian Weeks, a political scientist at the University of Michigan, says, "While trusting your gut may be beneficial in some situations, it turns out that putting faith in intuition over evidence leaves us susceptible to misinformation."

We No Longer Trust the Experts

The growing acceptance of fake news and other lies has led some commentators to say that Americans are living in a post-truth era. In this environment, opinions or feelings are more important than truth, in which some people believe whatever their ideological leaders say, even if it contradicts the facts. In such an environment, "truth" becomes conditional—it depends on who is speaking. Facts become irrelevant.

When someone presents opinions as the truth, facts—and opinions from experts on that matter—become less valued. This devaluing of expertise provides fertile ground for the spreading of fake news. If we believe only the people we follow on social media, we are apt to disbelieve experts who hold opposing views. The issue of climate change again provides a good example. Almost all scientists believe that Earth's climate is warming and that the causes are human-made. That's the expert opinion. Climate change deniers, however, say that this expert opinion is wrong, even though the deniers do not have the same education, experience, or data as the scientists. Whom should you believe—the informed experts or the uninformed laypersons? According to surveys, millions of people believe the fake news that climate change is not real. For them, expert scientific knowledge has become unimportant and the "truth" lies elsewhere.

In the post-truth environment, fake news is just as—if not more—trusted than real news, and expertise and experience in traditional journalism is diminished. Is the respected and established *New York Times* more accurate than the biased and often fact-free Infowars website? Yes, but Infowars readers don't agree. For those who follow

A woman and child walk through the flooded streets of Dhaka, Bangladesh, after a storm. According to climate scientists, rising global temperatures are creating more powerful storms and devastating floods. Yet many people believe fake science that claims climate change is a hoax. They no longer trust the experts.

and believe the conspiracy theories on Infowars, that site appears more truthful than the reporting that might disagree with it in the *Times*. "Truth" becomes dependent on whether and how much you believe the source. "The problem today is not that there aren't good news outlets; the problem is that there is a large group of Americans who don't believe what those outlets say, and have aggressively embraced an alternate, self-contained set of facts and sources of facts," says Jay Stanley, a senior policy analyst with the American Civil Liberties Union (ACLU, a national organization that defends the constitutional and legal rights and freedoms of US citizens).

As more people trust less expert sources, some traditional news organizations struggle to attract a paying audience and stay in business. And the more readers get their news from those with no journalistic training or experience, the more we devalue the expertise of journalists and open the door to disinformation and fake news. If we don't trust the real experts, then anyone can say anything and someone, somewhere will believe it.

We Like the Echo Chamber

Fake news spreads with remarkable speed and efficiency on the internet and through social media. And many people filter their news feeds to see only posts and stories they want to see. They avoid or block the opinions of those with whom they disagree. So people are less likely to be aware of information and opinions that differ from their views.

Some experts say this creates a kind of echo chamber, in which people hear their own opinions echoed back to them repeatedly. If you're a political conservative, you may listen only to right-wing talk radio, watch Fox News, and read and subscribe to various conservative-leaning websites and blogs. All these sources repeat the same headlines, talking points, and analysis. If you're a political liberal, you might seek only left-leaning media in which the same stories are repeated on multiple websites and blogs. Together, they reinforce the same viewpoint.

We Believe Things We Hear More Often

Social media connections are a thickly entangled web, with users often connected to the same people and to people with similar views. So it's not unusual to see the same stories and information multiple times. Facebook friends or Twitter followers may see a story on the Fox News website or the *New York Times* site and then repost it for others to see. Studies show that the more often people hear a piece of information, the more likely they are to believe it—even if the information is false. The simple act of repetition can eventually lead people to believe a story or statement they might otherwise distrust.

Social scientists call this the illusory truth effect. Put simply, people tend to view statements they've seen before as true. As psychologist Lisa Fazio of Vanderbilt University in Tennessee says, the more you hear something, the more "you'll have this gut-level feeling that maybe it's true." Gord Pennycook, a psychologist at Yale University in Connecticut adds, "Even things that people have reason not to believe, they believe them more" if the claims are repeated often enough.

During his presidential campaign in 2016, Donald Trump promised repeatedly to crack down on violent crime in the United States. He suggested that such crime is on an upswing. News broadcasts and social media platforms also give extensive coverage to violent crimes, so a person consuming this might think that violent crime is rising. But, according to both the FBI and the Bureau of Justice Statistics, violent crime in the United States has been steadily falling since the early 1990s. So has property crime such as theft. But we don't hear these statistics nearly as often as we hear about violent crime from Trump, the 24/7 news cycle, and social media. The misconception of rising crime becomes an illusory truth that "feels right" but is actually false.

We Share False Information More Often Than True Information

A massive study from researchers at the Massachusetts Institute of Technology (MIT) near Boston examined 126,000 stories shared on Twitter between 2006 and 2017. About three million people tweeted these stories more than 4.5 million times. The MIT researchers classified the stories as either true or false based on the opinions of six independent fact-checking organizations.

The researchers found that false stories spread significantly faster and to more people than did true stories—and certain types of false news spread even faster than other types. While all categories of false information spread quickly, false political news spread farther and faster than similarly false news about terrorism, natural disasters, science, or finance.

Why this fascination for false stories over true ones? The researchers speculate that false news is often more interesting and exciting than real news. They found that false stories are more likely to inspire strong emotions such as fear, disgust, and surprise. True stories tend to inspire softer emotions such as sadness, joy, and trust. People are more likely to share stories that lead to strong emotions.

DON'T BELIEVE EVERYTHING YOU SEE

You've probably heard this warning: don't believe anything unless you see it with your own two eyes. But as it becomes easier (and cheaper) to manipulate photos and videos digitally, you might not be able to believe your own eyes after all.

Since the late twentieth century, computer users have turned to editing programs such as Photoshop to alter digital photographs in subtle and obvious ways. Often subtle editing is used to touch up portraits in ads, magazine covers, and other media. Graphic artists can remove blemishes, even out skin tones, and make someone look thinner. These changes are usually to make an image more appealing to attract buyers.

Governments sometimes use photographic manipulation for propaganda. For instance, a campaign staffer working to reelect President George W. Bush in 2004 digitally altered a photograph of the president at a rally. The staffer copied and pasted sections of a different crowd scene into the image of Bush at the rally. This made the crowd of supporters behind Bush appear larger than it actually was.

With video editing programs, it's possible to work on entire videos, deleting people or objects from scenes and inserting people or objects into scenes. An editor can even make people appear to say or do things they didn't actually say or do in the original video. The doctored videos look real enough to convince viewers that they're seeing an accurate recording of events as they happened. Sometimes it's almost impossible to distinguish these digitally altered videos from the real thing.

Political Affiliation Makes a Difference

The willingness to believe fake news differs significantly by political orientation. Studies have shown that in general, Republicans are more susceptible to fake news—and less trusting of the traditional media—than are Democrats.

A 2017 survey by Gallup and the Knight Foundation asked more than nineteen thousand Americans to rate whether they always, sometimes, or never viewed four categories of information as fake news. The four categories were

1. false information deliberately portrayed as true
2. news stories for which journalists hadn't checked all their facts and sources
3. stories slanted to promote a certain viewpoint
4. news that someone simply found disagreeable

The survey also asked people whether they were a Democrat or Republican. Members of both parties generally agreed that the first category usually counted as fake news. But they disagreed on the other three categories. For example, Republicans were more likely to label news they disagreed with as fake than were Democrats. Republicans were also more likely to label news they perceived as politically biased as fake.

A 2017 poll by Politico and Morning Consult showed that 46 percent of US voters believed that the news media made up stories about Trump. Only 37 percent thought that the media did not make up stories. Political orientation skewed the results: 76 percent of Republican voters said that the news media made up stories, while only 20 percent of Democrats (and 44 percent of independent voters) believed this.

Education level plays into the equation. Another 2017 Gallup survey found that 49 percent of college graduates say the media generally get the facts straight, while just 28 percent of those with only a high school education agreed with that statement. But the numbers change when you consider political affiliation: 72 percent of Democrats with a college degree agree that news organizations are generally accurate. In contrast, only 18 percent of college-educated Republicans trust the accuracy of the media.

Why are Republicans more distrustful of news media than Democrats? It's a relatively recent phenomenon. Throughout most of the twentieth century, citizens of all political persuasions thought that newspapers and radio and television newscasts offered largely impartial reporting. The current conservative mistrust of mainstream media started with the rise of right-wing talk radio (led by Rush Limbaugh's syndicated radio show) in the late 1980s. It picked up steam with the launch of the right-leaning Fox News network in 1996. With a clear conservative voice on the airwaves, Republicans were free to question or completely abandon more neutral news sources. Those neutral sources were then viewed as left-leaning by the right-wing media, and the Republican mistrust of mainstream media began. This mistrust became more entrenched in the twenty-first century thanks to the echo chamber effect of social media.

As conservatives grew to rely more on their own right-wing media (and to distrust mainstream media), they became more susceptible to fake news that mirrored their political opinions. This is a key reason why conservatives are more likely to believe and share fake news stories than are liberals, who tend to trust and consume news from mainstream news organizations that offer a diversity of viewpoints.

CHAPTER 6

HOW HARMFUL IS FAKE NEWS?

At first, fake news can seem relatively harmless. Who's going to believe that the US government staged the moon landing in a Hollywood studio or that Bigfoot is prowling the local forests? And so what if people believe it? It doesn't harm anybody, does it?

True, stories about Bigfoot are usually harmless, but other fake news can cause real harm. Certain kinds of fake news can hurt people's careers, reputations, and safety. Fake news also puts democratic institutions, such as the free press and free and fair elections, at risk.

People Are Fooled—and Stay Fooled

The most obvious damage that flows from fake news is that some people really are fooled by it, and they tend to act according to the false facts they believe. For example, a person who believes that climate change is a conspiracy theory is unlikely to support government policies that discourage the use of fossil fuels. That person is unlikely to favor higher taxes on gasoline and lower taxes on alternative energy, such as solar power. That person probably won't vote for politicians who want to try to halt or slow climate change. And if some people believe that vaccines cause autism, they may refuse vaccinations for themselves and their children. Unvaccinated children and adults can catch infectious, sometimes life-threatening diseases and spread them to others. Vaccine

Members of the anti-Muslim group Act for America protest against sharia (Islamic) law at the Pennsylvania state capitol in 2017. Many fake news websites spread anti-Muslim propaganda, including the false news that American Muslims want to impose their religious law on US society.

resistance has led to disease outbreaks around the world, has enabled the resurgence of diseases previously eliminated from certain regions, and sometimes has led to deaths of unvaccinated children and adults. So fake news not only isn't harmless—it can be deadly.

Fake science can also physically harm people. Many popular fake science stories claim to offer a cure for cancer through a natural treatment. People who have cancer sometimes believe these stories. This is especially likely if they have incurable cancer, if they are dying, or if they don't trust traditional doctors. Some people will abandon medically supervised cancer treatments and start taking so-called "natural" supplements. But abandoning established medicine for fake solutions isn't a good idea. Even if the bogus cure doesn't kill people, it won't cure them.

Fake News and Violence

Some types of fake news can lead to violence—and sometimes death. This happened in the Southeast Asian nation of Myanmar (also known as Burma). Most people there practice the Buddhist religion, and a small minority are Muslim. In 2014 a radical Buddhist monk posted a false story on Facebook, charging that Muslim men had raped a Buddhist woman in the nation's second-largest city, Mandalay. This rumor spread quickly and sparked attacks on Muslims there. Rioters killed two people, injured dozens, ransacked Muslim-owned shops, and burned down a local mosque (Islamic place of worship).

Another example occurred during the 2016 presidential election. A fake news story claimed that the New York City Police Department had discovered a child sex-trafficking ring operating out of the basement in Comet Ping Pong, a Washington, DC–based pizzeria. The story claimed that presidential candidate Hillary Clinton and her campaign manager, John Podesta, were running the ring. Originally posted on Twitter, the story was false. The Comet Ping Pong pizza restaurant does operate in the nation's capital, but it was never the headquarters for sex-trafficking operations. Clinton and Podesta had no ties to the pizza parlor or sex trafficking. Clinton has been a vocal and longtime supporter of efforts to stop sex-trafficking and other forms of human trafficking. The original tweet was retweeted more than six thousand times. Eventually multiple right-wing message boards, blogs, Twitter, and Facebook feeds picked it up. It even got top billing on many fake news websites, which helped the unfounded rumor spread even farther. Before long, the mainstream media was covering the rumor.

> **"From this insane, fabricated conspiracy theory, we've come under constant assault."**
>
> —James Alefantis, whose restaurant was targeted in a fake news story

The story, dubbed Pizzagate, harmed the reputations of Podesta and Clinton. It also affected the restaurant and its staff. Within days of the fake story going live, the restaurant's owner and employees received hundreds of death threats from people on Facebook, Instagram, Reddit, Twitter, and YouTube. The restaurant's owner, James Alefantis, told the *New York Times*, "From this insane, fabricated conspiracy theory, we've come under constant assault. . . . I've done nothing for days but try to clean this up and protect my staff and friends from being terrorized."

The threats became real when Edgar Maddison Welch, a twenty-eight-year-old from North Carolina, visited the restaurant in person—with an AR-15-style assault rifle. He said he wanted to "self-investigate" the claims he had read online. After entering the pizzeria, he fired three rounds but hit no one. Welch was arrested and later convicted of assault with a dangerous weapon.

Labeling legitimate news as fake can also lead to threats of violence. In January 2018, after many months of Trump calling CNN a fake news medium, CNN offices received twenty-two threatening phone calls—all from the same person. The caller allegedly told CNN operators, "Fake news. I'm coming to gun you all down," and "I'm coming for you, CNN. . . . Your cast is about to get gunned down in a matter of hours."

CNN alerted authorities, and the FBI traced the calls to nineteen-year-old Michigan resident Brandon Griesemer. The FBI arrested him before he acted on his threats.

People Distrust the Media

At one time, Americans put great trust in TV news reporters such as Walter Cronkite. Cronkite was a much-beloved anchor on the *CBS Evening News* from 1962 to 1981. With his deep voice and caring personality, he was trusted and respected by most Americans. But trust in the news media has greatly declined. According to

Gallup polls, trust in the media peaked in 1976; Americans felt that journalists had proven their value and done the nation a great service by exposing corruption in the administration of President Richard Nixon. Then, according to Gallup, 72 percent of Americans felt they had a "great deal" or "fair amount" of trust in the media. But by 2016, just 32 percent of Americans claimed to have a "great deal" or "fair amount" of trust in the media.

This decline in trust has been going on for a long time and for many reasons. They include the growing political polarization in the United States, the rise of biased news sources, the increase of opinion-based content on broadcast news, and a growing distrust in other established US institutions, such as churches, big business, and Congress. This suspicion of the media has accelerated even more since the rise of fake news. With so much fake news circulating, people don't

CBS news anchor Walter Cronkite delivers the news on TV in 1969. Most Americans at the time trusted the news media and viewed national news anchors with reverence and deep respect.

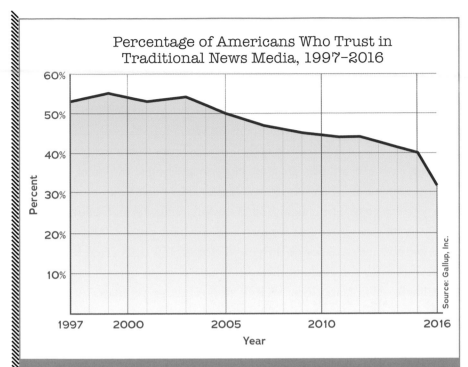

Percentage of Americans Who Trust in Traditional News Media, 1997–2016

Source: Gallup, Inc.

The number of Americans saying they have a "great deal" or "fair amount" of trust in the news media has declined since 1997.

know what news organizations to believe—and when they don't know what to believe, they begin to doubt and distrust all media.

This lack of trust in the media increases the more people perceive the media to be biased. The Pew Research Center reported in 2017 that 72 percent of Americans believe that news organizations tend to favor only one side of the political spectrum—either right or left, but not both. And many Americans distrust this narrow coverage, especially if it represents a point of view they don't share.

Politicians who repeatedly cry "fake news" with every story they don't like contribute to the mistrust of media. This is especially true when the claim of fake news is itself false. And research shows that constant attacks that repeat the same thing tend to become believable over time. So even a false charge of fake news can seem true.

Undermining Democracy

The result of this distrust is that citizens become confused, less informed, and increasingly cynical. A 2016 research study by Stanford University in California found that a majority of young students can't tell the difference between sponsored content, politically biased messages on social media, and factual news. If people don't know which news to trust, they are more likely to accept one version of the story, without doing any checking. Or they might just tune out the news completely. They might stop discussing politics with friends, give up on voting, and lose faith in the democratic process. And when people no longer exercise their rights as citizens in a democracy, it becomes easier for would-be dictators to take over the government. As happened in Nazi Germany, legislators might propose laws that condemn or punish a certain minority group or that strip citizens of their rights. If citizens aren't paying attention, monitoring the behavior of elected representatives, communicating with them, and voting for or against them, then such laws might pass.

The drip, drip, drip of fake news stories and attacks on the legitimate news media can have a devastating long-term effect. Democracy—especially representative democracy (in which people vote for fellow citizens to represent them in legislatures and other decision-making bodies)—depends on trust. People in democratic societies such as the United States have to trust that elected leaders are acting in the best interests of the people they represent. When leaders deliberately lie, it undermines trust in them and in the democratic system. A free press plays an important role in holding leaders accountable and exposing them if they are dishonest or corrupt. The system breaks down if those in power challenge the truthfulness of the press, try to shut it down, or try to censor it. Thomas Jefferson (1743–1826), the third president of the United States, wrote in 1786, "Our liberty depends on the freedom of the press, and that cannot be limited without being lost."

THE FOUNDERS
AND THE PRESS

The founders of the United States of America or, in some cases, their ancestors had migrated to North America from Britain, a country with a history of strong restrictions on the press. For example, in 1538 England's King Henry VIII issued a law that all printed materials, including newspapers and books, must be licensed and approved by his government. The law eliminated any negative press about the king or his top officials.

Britain's press was further muzzled by the similar Licensing of the Press Act of 1662, which required Parliament (the British lawmaking body) to license printers and printing presses for the production of books, pamphlets, newspapers, and other media. The goal was to stop the spread of antigovernment ideas, and the result was that the number of British newspapers was reduced to just one, the pro-government *London Gazette*.

After the law expired in 1692, several new newspapers were founded, but the British press was still severely restricted. Other laws made it a criminal offense to print anything negative about the king, the government, or Parliament or to print anything that would encourage citizens to overthrow the government. Again, the laws had the effect of muzzling any criticism of the government or king.

Knowing that a vibrant and free press was essential to the success of their burgeoning democracy, the US founders wanted to distance themselves from such press prohibitions. This led to the codification of press freedoms in the First Amendment to the Constitution and a strong defense of the press by Thomas Jefferson and other founders.

A press that is free of censorship and government control ensures that all reporting—not just the official government version—is heard. An unrestricted press is a form of checks and balances to keep government accountable.

A free press is also important for sharing the voices of the people. In many autocratic nations, such as China, the government controls the press. Only the official government view is allowed in print, on the air, and online. The government censors dissenting opinions and may arrest and jail journalists who oppose the government's official party line. In some nations, including Russia and Mexico, the government might even kill reporters who write about corruption and misdeeds of government officials. According to the Committee to Protect Journalists, an international watchdog organization, 1,305 journalists worldwide have been murdered since 1992, including 18 in 2017. Powerful politicians who were displeased by the journalists' critical research and reporting likely hired people to kill them. When journalists fear for their lives, they might understandably stop working as reporters, enabling corrupt governments to continue without serious opposition.

Some nations also try to control what information their citizens can access over the internet. China, in particular, blocks access to websites that present viewpoints that the government doesn't want

> "The phrase 'fake news' . . . is being used by autocrats to silence reporters, undermine political opponents, stave off media scrutiny and mislead citizens."
>
> —US senator John McCain, 2018

people to see. China also sometimes jams citizen access to Western-based sites, such as Google and Facebook; shuts down video-streaming sites; requires users to use their real names when registering with online forums, so they can't anonymously criticize the government; and censors or punishes those who express antigovernment views. Such restrictions limit what China's 750 million internet users view online, keeps them from dissenting and protesting government misdeeds, and provides them with only a partial view of what's happening worldwide.

CHAPTER 7
FAKE NEWS AND FREE SPEECH

Fake news undermines public confidence in legitimate news sources. It sways people to believe things that aren't true—and to disbelieve things that are. It feeds on and promotes prejudice and paranoia, and it derails rational discussion. Fake news harms individuals and institutions and is a threat to democracy itself.

So why isn't fake news illegal? Shouldn't those who create and spread fake news face legal consequences? Shouldn't laws prohibit spreading rumor, innuendo, and falsehoods through the media?

The US Constitution says no. It protects freedom of speech. American colonists fought the Revolutionary War to free themselves of an oppressive British government that did not allow criticism of the country's government, rulers, or established church. The founders of the United States wanted to ensure that the new US government would not oppress its citizens by silencing their voices.

With the First Amendment to the Constitution, the founders guaranteed freedom of the press, freedom of speech, and freedom of religion. The amendment says, "Congress shall make no law respecting an establishment of religion, or prohibiting the free exercise thereof; or abridging the freedom of speech, or of the press; or the right of the people peaceably to assemble, and to petition the Government for a redress of grievances."

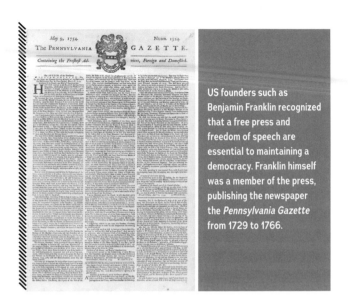

US founders such as Benjamin Franklin recognized that a free press and freedom of speech are essential to maintaining a democracy. Franklin himself was a member of the press, publishing the newspaper the *Pennsylvania Gazette* from 1729 to 1766.

What Is Free Speech?

US political leader Benjamin Franklin (1706–1790), a signer of the Constitution, wrote that there is "no such Thing as publick Liberty, without Freedom of Speech." During Franklin's lifetime, Americans expressed themselves through public speeches and written communications such as newspapers, books, broadsides, and pamphlets. In the twenty-first century, "speech" also includes information in magazines, radio, television, films, video games, and the internet.

Because the Constitution guarantees freedom of speech, Americans have the right to freely exchange all types of ideas—even controversial or false ones. In the years since the nation's founding, the Supreme Court has ruled that the First Amendment protects anonymous speech, political speech, religious speech, and speech critical of the government. According to the court, the First Amendment even protects hate speech, or speech that attacks a person or group based on their race, ethnicity, religion, gender, sexual

THE FAIRNESS DOCTRINE

The First Amendment protects free speech. Some exceptions apply for broadcast radio and television stations (such as ABC, NBC, and CBS). These stations lease bandwidth (a range of airwaves, which carry radio and television signals) from the US government and must be licensed to use this bandwidth. And the Federal Communications Commission (FCC) imposes certain regulations on the content of what the stations air. For example, the FCC does not allow broadcast TV to air pornography or other obscene content.

The rules about political stories on broadcast TV and radio have changed over time. Introduced in 1949, the Fairness Doctrine required holders of broadcast licenses to present controversial issues in a fair and balanced fashion. For example, the FCC's equal-time rule required broadcasters to provide equal time to candidates of opposing political parties. The goal was to avoid favoring one candidate over another so that stations could not sway public opinion or influence election results unfairly.

In 1987 the FCC overturned the Fairness Doctrine, stating that it violated First Amendment free speech rights and did not serve the public's interest. Without the doctrine, television and radio broadcasts could and did become more partisan, moving to the right or left end of the political spectrum. This resulted in an upsurge in politically polarized radio and television programs, especially from conservative voices such as Rush Limbaugh and Glenn Beck.

Some critics have blamed the rise of hyperpartisan politics and ugly speech on the repeal of the Fairness Doctrine. Congress has tried to bring back the Fairness Doctrine, but the attempts all failed. In 2011 the FCC pulled the doctrine from its official rule book.

orientation, or other attributes. The government cannot shut down the right to free speech. For this reason, it is not against the law to create and spread misleading or untruthful stories.

But the Supreme Court has also ruled that some types of speech do not have First Amendment protection. These include child pornography, fighting words (challenging someone to a fight), perjury (lying in court), blackmail, threatening to harm someone, and inciting others to (encouraging) violence or criminal acts. Spreading fake news and other misinformation does not clearly fall into any of these categories. So it is not a crime to create or spread fake news.

Limitations on Free Speech Rights

While protecting many types of speech, the Supreme Court has also put some limits on free speech.. For example, the US Supreme Court ruled in 1919 in *Schenck v. United States* that the First Amendment does not protect false speech that is meant to cause harm to others. Justice Oliver Wendell Holmes wrote,

> The most stringent [strictest] protection of free speech would not protect a man in falsely shouting fire in a theatre and causing a panic. . . . The question in every case is whether the words used are used in such circumstances and are of such a nature as to create a clear and present danger.

Therefore, another person's right to safety overrides the right to freedom of expression.

Can the Government Outlaw Fake News?

Some lawmakers have suggested making laws to prohibit fake news. For example, in March 2017, in response to charges of Russian interference in the 2016 presidential election, Democratic California state legislator Ed Chau introduced the California Political Cyberfraud Abatement Act.

DEFENDING THE FIRST AMENDMENT

Dedicated to defending the First Amendment, the American Civil Liberties Union has filed a number of lawsuits in defense of controversial and hateful speech. For example, several times in the 1930s and 1940s, the ACLU defended the right of the Ku Klux Klan, an American white supremacist group, to hold rallies. In the late 1970s, the ACLU defended the right of the neo-Nazi, Chicago-based Nationalist Socialist Party of America to hold a demonstration in Skokie, Illinois. The group was planning to carry its flag, which has the image

Protesters and counterprotesters clash at a white supremacist rally in Charlottesville, Virginia, in 2017. The US Supreme Court has ruled that the First Amendment protects hateful speech. In the case of Charlottesville, however, some demonstrators carried weapons and one counterprotester was killed. Some constitutional scholars say that First Amendment rights should not extend to violent demonstrations such as this one.

of the Nazi swastika, a powerful symbol of hatred of Jews. Skokie, in suburban Chicago, is home to many Jews who had been terrorized by Nazis or survived the Holocaust during World War II. The neo-Nazi group chose the location on purpose, to inflame the populace. The group didn't hold the march, despite court decisions allowing it. And in 2017, the ACLU defended the right of white supremacists—some wielding weapons—to hold a protest in Charlottesville, Virginia.

In these cases, the ACLU argued that the government can't control speech based on the content of that speech, no matter how vile or objectionable it is. However, after the protest in Charlottesville turned violent, with one person killed, the ACLU faced backlash for defending the rights of hate groups. The ACLU reacted to this criticism by announcing that it would no longer support armed hate groups in situations that are likely to turn violent. This is a major change in direction for the ACLU. It still supports First Amendment free speech rights in general, but not the right to hold potentially violent protests.

Many Americans want to see more regulation of speech, specifically fake news, on social media platforms. So far, the ACLU objects to any restrictions. The ACLU's Jay Stanley said in 2016, "A forum for free expression that is as central to our national political conversations as Facebook [should] not feature any kind of censorship or other interference with the neutral flow of information." In the ACLU's eyes, the right to free speech online takes precedence over any attempt, no matter how well intentioned, to regulate demonstrably fake news and information.

Chau wanted to assure that upcoming US elections would not be vulnerable to the type of fraud, hacking, and other meddling seen in 2016. Chau's bill would have added the following to California's election code:

> It is unlawful for a person to knowingly and willingly make, publish or circulate on an Internet Web site, or cause to be made, published, or circulated in any writing posted on an Internet Web site, a false or deceptive statement designed to influence the vote on either of the following:
>
> (e) Any issue submitted to voters at an election.
> (f) Any candidate for election to public office.

Free speech advocacy groups such as the nonprofit Electronic Frontier Foundation in San Francisco opposed this and similar legislation. The foundation said that the bill's wording was so general that it would have banned many types of political speech, including satirical articles from the *Onion* and *Saturday Night Live* skits. The unintended consequences of the law would likely have outweighed the intended benefits. Lawmakers in California agreed, so the bill never went up for a vote in the state's assembly.

Trying to control fake news is a double-edged sword. Free speech advocates say that if the government tries to ban fake news, free speech will suffer. And in a democracy, it is important to protect even disdainful opinions. Restricting speech that we do not like can have a chilling effect on citizens. Individuals become afraid to voice their opinions for fear of arrest. This is what happened in Nazi Germany and still happens in countries such as Russia and Turkey, where journalists and other critics of the government often are jailed for reporting negative stories about leaders and the ruling classes.

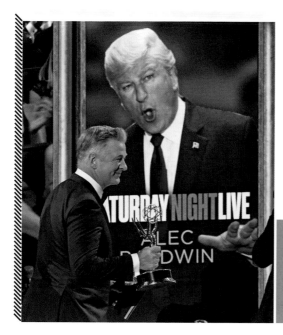

Actor Alec Baldwin receives an Emmy Award for impersonating Donald Trump on *Saturday Night Live*. The right to free speech includes the right to poke fun at politicians.

What Can Victims Do?

With so many types of speech protected by the First Amendment, do victims of fake news have any legal recourse? Yes. The Supreme Court has ruled that citizens can sue another party for libel (also known as defamation): a written, published, or broadcast statement that is obviously false and that damages another person in some way. Damage may include hurting the person's reputation, causing embarrassment, or causing the person to lose a job. Citizens can also sue for slander, a spoken false statement that also damages another person in one of these ways.

So if you are a victim of a fake news story and you can prove that the story caused harm to you, you can sue the person who wrote that story or the organization that published it for libel. To prove harm, the plaintiff (the person bringing legal action) must show that a person or organization has published or broadcast something they know to be false about the plaintiff. However, proving that the defendant knew

FAKE NEWS OVERSEAS

Fake news is not just a US phenomenon. Fake news stories have also influenced elections and spread rumors and hate speech in Europe and elsewhere.

Some foreign lawmakers hope to stop the spread of fake news online. For instance, in April 2017, German lawmakers introduced a bill to force social media companies such as Facebook and Twitter to quickly remove fake news posts that incite hate or that include criminal content. The punishment for not removing the posts would be a fine as high as 50 million euros (about $58 million).

Opponents of the legislation feared it would limit free speech and the legitimate press. Yet people who favored it saw a need to counter the growing problem of fake news and hate speech on German social networks—particularly hate speech against Muslim immigrants in Germany. As German justice minister Heiko Maas said in support of the bill, "The providers of social networks are responsible when their platforms are misused to spread hate crime or illegal false news." The law passed and went into effect in 2018.

When he was Germany's justice minister, Heiko Maas spearheaded the law to remove hate speech from German social media.

the information was false is not enough. The plaintiff must also be able to prove that the false information has caused harm, financial or otherwise.

Libel is a civil action—a legal dispute between two private citizens or organizations. Libel is not a criminal case—a case in which the defendant, if found guilty of breaking the law, would be punished by the state.

One high-profile libel case involving fake news happened in April 2017. Chobani, a company that produces and sells a popular Greek yogurt, sued radio show host Alex Jones for defamation. Jones is a conspiracy theorist who runs the Infowars website, which publishes anti-immigrant propaganda, fake news, urban legends, and the like to a mostly right-wing audience. Jones had published stories and videos on Infowars, Twitter, and YouTube falsely claiming that child rape and a tuberculosis outbreak had taken place at Chobani's food processing plant in Twin Falls, Idaho. "Idaho Yogurt Maker Caught Importing Migrant Rapists" was one of the videos. Believing these stories, some customers threatened to boycott (refuse to buy) Chobani yogurt.

Chobani sued Jones and Infowars for libel. The yogurt company sought to prove that the false stories and the threat of boycott had caused it financial harm. Rather than go to court, which is expensive and time consuming, Jones agreed to settle the suit for an undisclosed amount of money. He also admitted that "certain statements were made on the Infowars, Twitter feed and YouTube channel regarding Chobani, LLC that I now understand to be wrong. . . . On behalf of Infowars, I regret that we mischaracterized Chobani, its employee and the people of Twin Falls, Idaho, the way we did."

CHAPTER 8
HOW TO TELL FAKE NEWS FROM REAL NEWS

Many fake news stories are just close enough to the truth to seem legitimate. In social media feeds, fake stories are there alongside legitimate stories. People you know and trust often share the phony stories. So do some cable news and talk radio programs. People in power also attack genuine news stories they don't like as fake news. It's becoming more and more difficult to distinguish the fake news from the factual news.

So how do we do that? When you don't know whom or what to believe, you have to do your own homework to separate fact from fiction. This means getting more involved with what you view online, see or hear on broadcast media, and read in print. You are the ultimate fact-checker.

What Fake News Looks Like

Fake news, when done well, looks a lot like real news. If you're reading a story on a fake news website, it will have a headline, a main article, and sometimes an accompanying photo—just like a story on a hard news site. If you're reading a fake post on Facebook or other social media, it will look like any other post.

How do you separate fact from fiction on social media? Do some basic research and use common sense to figure out what is reliable information and what is not.

To determine if the story is fact or fiction, start by examining the fake news headline. Compared to news stories from reputable sources, fake news headlines tend to be sensational. Consider the following two news headlines. Do they seem a little over the top to you?

- $4 Million and 2 Dead Bodies Found in Democrat Mayor's Storage Unit
- Morgue Employee Cremated by Mistake While Taking a Nap

They are over the top, and they're both fake. Yet many legitimate news sources also print sensational headlines, known as clickbait. These headlines attract curious readers and advertising clicks. For example, these headlines for real news stories might seem as unbelievable as those headlines for a typical fake news story:

- Donald Trump Campaign Offered Actors $50 to Cheer for Him at Presidential Announcement

- Elephants Deserve Legal "Personhood," New Lawsuit Argues in Connecticut
- "Grumpy Cat" Wins $700,000 in Federal Case Over Identity
- Man Shoots Armadillo but Accidentally Hits His Mother-in-Law
- Man Swept out to Sea During Sunday Morning Baptism

All these headlines sound outrageous, but the stories are true. So you can't always tell a fake news story by how ridiculous it sounds. But a sensational headline is often a red flag that a story may be false.

Be wary also of headlines with exaggerated claims, words in all capital letters, or words with exclamation points. The article's writer is trying to garner an emotional response. Legitimate news sources typically do not use these techniques.

More Red Flags

Many fake news sites are designed to look like legitimate news sites—and to fool site visitors. You can often spot these sites by their URLs. For example, the real CBS News website is at www.cbsnews.com, but for a while, a fake news site operated at www.cbsnews.com.co. People who weren't paying close attention thought they were visiting CBS News at that address but were getting fake news. So check the URL of a website for signs it may not be legitimate. Also look for .co or .om at the end of the URL (instead of the more common .com). Look for misspellings of a legitimate site name—"washingtonpoast.com" instead of "washingtonpost.com," for example.

In the article itself, look for misspellings and incorrect grammar. Many fake stories are written by non-English speakers, and they contain many language errors. Next, look at the data contained in the article. Many fake news stories present just one piece of evidence, such as survey results, a statement from an expert, or a hacked document, to support the entire article. In real journalism, serious claims are supported by multiple sources, not a single source. Read the article all the way through to the end. Does the article cite its sources, naming specific scholars, universities, government agencies, or other entities that contributed data? Or is information presented as true without any background or sources provided?

Examine any photos accompanying the article. Many fake news articles include sexually suggestive, bizarre, or disturbing images—many of them obviously doctored. After looking at the pictures, examine the site hosting the article. Do the other articles on the site appear to be legitimate, or are they also suspect? Does the site have an "About" section where you can learn more about the hosting organization and whether it deals in legitimate news? Is it a reputable source that you're familiar with, such as a national newspaper or well-known media website? Or is it a source you've never heard of?

While you're looking at the source, also look for the story's reporter or writer. Search for other stories written by that person. If your search turns up many well-researched stories in reputable publications, then the story you're checking on is probably real. If the reporter hasn't written any other stories or if no reporter is listed, then the story could be fake.

Make sure that the story is widely reported. Open your web browser and do a Google search to see if you can find a similar story from another source. If you can't find any corroborating stories, the original story is likely a fake. If you do find similar stories, but

> **In real journalism, serious claims are supported by multiple sources, not a single source.**

they're all from similarly questionable sources, that too signals a fake. But if you find similar stories from trusted sources—including sources across all media, such as television and print—then the story is probably true.

To help you separate fact from fiction, several websites specialize in debunking fake news, urban legends, and conspiracy theories. The most popular of these sites is Snopes (www.snopes.com), a reliable source for fact-checking questionable news posts you find online. You can browse there for debunked or confirmed stories and search for information about a particular item.

If you want to determine the truthfulness of a political news item, use PolitiFact (www.politifact.com). PolitiFact relies on a team of staffers to research and determine the accuracy of statements from elected officials, politicians, and pundits. Accuracy is rated on the site's Truth-O-Meter, in degrees from True to False.

How to Identify Reputable News Sources

If you see an item from CNN, ABC News, or the Associated Press, it's real news. However, if the item comes from a source that is less well known or not known to you at all, investigate further.

To figure out whether a news source is trustworthy, biased, or fake, visit Media Bias/Fact Check (www.mediabiasfactcheck.com). This site lists most known major media outlets, online and off-line, and ranks them according to perceived bias. Enter the name of the website or organization to see whether it has a leftward bias, has a right-leaning bias, or is relatively unbiased. You can also find out whether a site promotes conspiracy theories or pseudoscience (fake science).

Another good test is to see whether the news outlet has an ombudsman or public editor to handle consumer complaints and criticisms. Similarly, check to see how the source handles mistakes. If a source is open to self-examination and freely issues corrections when it gets the facts wrong, you can trust it.

Examining Trusted Sources

Bias is hard to escape, but most mainstream media are more balanced than many political diehards would like people to believe. Some conservatives talk about the "lamestream media," criticizing its alleged liberal bias. But various studies show that most major national newspapers, magazines, websites, and news channels are pretty accurate in reporting the daily news. Bob Schieffer, former anchor of *CBS Evening News* and former host of CBS's *Face the Nation*, says that "what drives the vast majority of reporters is not a hidden political agenda, but simply a desire to get the story and to get it before their competitors."

> "What drives the vast majority of reporters is not a hidden political agenda, but simply a desire to get the story and to get it before their competitors."
>
> —Bob Schieffer, former anchor of *CBS Evening News* and former host of CBS's *Face the Nation*

In general, traditional news gathering organizations such as the Associated Press and Bloomberg are relatively unbiased and present verifiable facts. So are traditional network news organizations (ABC, CBS, and NBC) and major national newspapers (the *New York Times*, *Wall Street Journal*, and *Washington Post*). Other organizations, such as *Slate* and the *National Review*, are more leftward or rightward leaning, respectively. They still focus on reporting facts not opinion.

The following table, based on data from mediabiaschart.com, lays out the well-known biases of several popular, established US and international news sources:

Type of bias	News sources
Strong liberal bias	Alternet, Daily Beast, Daily Kos, HuffPost, the Intercept, *Mother Jones*, *New Republic*, Salon, Slate
Slight liberal bias	*Atlantic*, BuzzFeed, MSNBC, the *Nation*, *New Yorker*, Politico, *Vanity Fair*, Vox
Minimal bias	ABC News, Agence France-Press, Al Jazeera, Associated Press, Bloomberg, British Broadcasting Corporation, CBS News, *Christian Science Monitor*, CNN, *Guardian*, National Public Radio, NBC News, *New York Times*, Public Broadcasting Service, Reuters, *Time*, USA Today, *Wall Street Journal* (news section), *Washington Post*
Slight conservative bias	*Economist*, the *Hill*, *National Review*, *Wall Street Journal* (editorial pages), *Weekly Standard*
Strong conservative bias	Daily Caller, Drudge Report, Fox News, Newsmax, *New York Post*, TheBlaze

As the table illustrates, many biased sources report on the news. But reporting in general tends to gravitate to the middle of the political spectrum.

News sources also differ by the mix of hard news and opinion that they publish. For example, major national newspapers present more news than opinion. Major cable news organizations (CNN, Fox News, and MSNBC) present more opinion than fact. Other sources, such as the blog *Patribotics* and Infowars, present much misleading or fabricated content. The following table, based on data from mediabiaschart.com, shows the breakdown:

Emphasis	News sources
Fact-based reporting	ABC News, Agence France-Press, Associated Press, Axios, Bloomberg, British Broadcasting Corporation, CBS News, the *Hill*, National Public Radio, NBC News, *New York Post*, Politico, Public Broadcasting Service, Reuters, *Time*, *Wall Street Journal*, *Washington Post*
Opinion and analysis	Alternet, BuzzFeed, CNN, Daily Kos, Drudge Report, *Economist*, Fox News, *Guardian*, the Intercept, *Mother Jones*, MSNBC, the *Nation*, *National Review*, *New Republic*, *New Yorker*, *New York Post*, Salon, Slate, *Weekly Standard*
Misleading or fabricated information	Breitbart, Daily Caller, Infowars, *National Enquirer*, Natural News, Newsmax, Occupy Democrats, *Patribotics*, Red State, TheBlaze

HOW SOCIAL MEDIA FIGHTS FAKE NEWS

Social media spreads a significant percentage of fake news, typically by people reposting false stories to their online friends. But Facebook, Twitter, and other social media have been slow to try to stop the spread of fake news. This is partly because their success depends in part on advertising revenues, and fake news posts generate a lot of advertising income.

Still, Facebook has tried several approaches to identify or remove obvious fake posts and propaganda from its site. Initially, Facebook tried to mark fake news stories with a red flag icon. But the company found that flagging a story actually encouraged people to read it. Since flagging backfired, the editorial staff at Facebook instead opted to include links to other, more trustworthy articles—dubbed "Related Articles"—under questionable posts. The hope is that users will click the links to read more reliable reporting on controversial topics. Facebook has found that the "Related Articles" tool has led to fewer shared fake stories. And if Facebook's fact-checkers classify a story as fake, it is demoted in users' news feeds. This makes the fake story harder for users to find and reduces its impact and spread.

Despite these efforts, many critics say that Facebook hasn't done enough. Some politicians, journalists, and others are disturbed by how fake news and Russian posts and advertising affected the US presidential election of 2016. In April 2018, Congress called Facebook founder and CEO Mark Zuckerberg to testify about several issues, including Russian election interference via Facebook. Zuckerberg apologized for Facebook's failure to stop Russian meddling. He noted that the company would be employing new artificial intelligence tools to detect and thwart such activity in future elections in the United States and around the world.

Twitter has been less aggressive than Facebook in fighting fake news. As of early 2018, Twitter hadn't introduced any concrete measures to flag or remove fake news items. The company is said to be investigating a tab to flag fake news items and machine learning, or artificial intelligence, to identify and remove bot accounts.

In April 2018, Facebook founder Mark Zuckerberg (*seated at the table*) spoke to Congress about his company's failure to protect private user data. He also testified about Russian interference through Facebook postings during the 2016 presidential election. Facebook has stepped up its efforts to detect and flag fake news. But critics say Facebook has a long way to go before it is a truly reliable and safe platform.

Surveys show that the American public trusts the least biased news sources more than those with known biases. For example, in 2017 the Reynolds Journalism Institute (a center for journalism research at the University of Missouri) asked 8,728 news consumers to reveal their top twenty most trusted news sources. The following list contains news organizations with primarily fact-based reporting and minimal known bias:

1. *Economist*
2. public television
3. Reuters
4. British Broadcasting Corporation
5. National Public Radio
6. Public Broadcasting Service
7. *Guardian*
8. *Wall Street Journal*
9. *Los Angeles Times*
10. *Dallas Morning News*
11. local news organizations
12. Politico
13. Associated Press
14. *Denver Post*
15. *Washington Post*
16. *Time* magazine
17. *Seattle Times*
18. *Kansas City Star*
19. *New York Times*
20. *USA Today*

According to the same report, the least trusted sources are these:

1. Occupy Democrats
2. BuzzFeed
3. Breitbart
4. social media in general

Know Your Own Biases

Perhaps you think that all talk radio shows are conservative mouthpieces or that all major newspapers are leftist propaganda outlets. If so, chances are that you are biased, not the sources. If you hold far-right views, anything to the left of your views might strike you as liberal—even if it's actually in the middle of the political spectrum. And if you're a liberal, anything to the right of your views might seem conservative. This is why Fox News viewers think the *New York Times* is liberal (it's not) and why MSNBC viewers think *USA Today* is conservative (it's not).

Just because reporting differs from your own viewpoint doesn't mean it's biased. And in spite of what some pundits claim, you really can trust the major news networks and the major national and international newspapers. They get it right more often than not.

CHAPTER 9

YOU CAN HELP FIGHT FAKE NEWS

Fake news wouldn't be a big issue if nobody shared it. But fake news *is* shared—a lot—and especially through social media. While there's not much you can do to stop the creation of fake news, you can help to stop its spread. Know how to recognize questionable news stories and then don't share them. To be responsible on social media, you must keep your news feed as factual as possible.

First, identify stories that are likely to be false. Look for items with outrageous headlines or obviously biased content. Be suspicious of items from unknown or disreputable news sources, stories without an identified author, and stories that link to sites with questionable URLs. Most important, when you find an item in your news feed that you think may be fake, don't repost it. By not spreading fake news, you can be part of the solution rather than part of the problem.

Read before You Share

Much of the spread of fake news occurs through irresponsible sharing. A 2016 study from Columbia University in New York City and Inria, a French technology institute, found that 59 percent of the news from links shared on social media wasn't read first. People see an intriguing headline or photo in their news feed or on another website and then click the Share button to repost the item to their social media friends—

without ever clicking through to the full article. Then they may be sharing fake news.

To stop the spread of fake news, read stories before you share them. Respect your social media friends enough to know what information you're sending their way. You may discover, on close inspection, that an article you were about to share is obviously fraudulent, that it doesn't really say what the headline promises, or that you actually disagree with it.

And when you do share information, online or off-line, cite your sources. Avoid posting or tweeting your own or others' opinions. Share only news from legitimate sources, and make those sources known. Be as responsible in your social sharing as you expect your friends to be.

Research the Source

Just because a friend or family member posts something on Facebook or Twitter doesn't make it true. The item has likely been shared hundreds or thousands of times, traveling from one person to the next.

Media literacy is part of the curriculum. The goal is to encourage and teach students how to evaluate and make decisions about the messages and information coming at them from electronic, TV, radio, and print sources. With tools for analyzing media (including social media), students can more easily separate real news from fake news.

It's not firsthand information. So it's important to do a little fact-checking to find out where the item was originally posted. If the item links to a website, click through to get the website name. You can then research the site to see if it publishes real or fake news.

If the source is not obvious, you may need to copy and paste the article's headline or first sentence into a search engine. The search may turn up multiple postings of the same story. Keep checking until you find the original posting. If the post is a real article from a legitimate source, such as the Associated Press or the *New York Times*, it's safe to share. But if it's propaganda or fake news from an unreliable source, stop the spread and don't share it with others. And follow a basic rule of thumb: when in doubt, don't repost.

Wait a Bit

When news breaks, it often comes with rumors, speculation, and misinformation, typically through social media. For example, during and immediately after a mass shooting at a country music concert in Las Vegas, Nevada, on October 1, 2017, rumors swirled around the internet. Some posts said that multiple shooters were involved. Others said the terrorist group ISIS inspired the shooting. Still others said that more shootings had taken place in other places in Las Vegas. None of these rumors were true, but in the confusion surrounding the event as it developed in real time, these and other "in the moment" posts quickly spread.

This situation occurs with any breaking news event, whether it's a school shooting, terrorist attack, or weather disaster. People want to know what's going on, and the fastest way to find out is online. Sometimes the information spread on social media is true and useful. Sometimes it is only hearsay and speculation.

So if something serious is unfolding, go online to see what you can find out. But don't necessarily take the first thing you read as the truth or the full story, especially if it's not from a reliable source. Over time,

Fake news often spreads quickly during and immediately after tragic events such as mass shootings. To get the facts, wait for formal press conferences and thorough reporting from the established news media. It may be a matter of hours, days, weeks, or even years before the full story is known. The important thing is to be patient as the story unfolds. Here, Texas governor Greg Abbott addresses the press after a shooting at Santa Fe High School in Santa Fe, Texas, in May 2018.

professional journalists will report more fully on the story, and you'll get accurate coverage by being patient. Equally important, don't share the first posts you read online. Even if they are from a trusted, reliable source, they are likely to be incomplete. Wait a bit. It might take a little time for all the facts to come out, especially during an unfolding event. Meanwhile, don't contribute to the misinformation by sharing too early and too quickly.

Correct Your Mistakes

It happens. Sometimes you share fake news. Everybody is tricked every now and then. If you post something that isn't factual and realize your mistake, delete the post. Even better, after deleting the original post, create a new post that explains what happened. Tell your friends that you discovered that a previous post shared fake information. It's okay to admit that you've made a mistake, and it's good to clear the air and make everyone aware of the danger of fake news.

Bottom line: to slow the spread of fake news, be careful about what you share on social media. A lot of phony information is out there. Don't be duped into sharing it. Maintain your own trustworthiness by recognizing fake news when you see it—and then not sharing it.

Debunk Misinformation with Facts

What do you do when a friend or family member persists in repeating and spreading fake news? While it is difficult to change a person's beliefs, you can refute obviously false information. But just labeling something a "lie" won't be enough. In 2017 a team of analysts from the University of Illinois and the University of Pennsylvania examined two decades of research on the topic of misinformation. They concluded that recipients of misinformation are less likely to accept countermessages when the argument is that the original information is "wrong." More success comes when you try to debunk information by providing new details not previously known to the other person.

So if someone you know believes the fake news that the streaks left in the sky by aircraft at high altitudes are made of chemicals designed to sicken the population, refer that person to articles from the US Air Force or the US Environmental Protection Agency explaining that the streaks, called contrails, contain only water vapor. Researchers have found that videos can be even more effective than printed materials in debunking false information. So if you can refer your friend to an online video about contrails from a respected scientific organization, the message might be more successfully received. Armed with new information, your friend might let go of the false claims and embrace the true ones.

Not all your efforts at debunking false stories will succeed. If some people truly believe the misinformation, counterarguments and new data might not change their minds.

Speak Up!

You do not have to stand idly by as social media, blogs, cable news networks, and talk radio shows spread fake news. You can express your opposition by writing letters and sending emails to the leaders and owners of these organizations, and by encouraging your friends to do so. You can also post your concerns about fake news on Facebook and Twitter for everyone to see.

You can encourage others to protest against and boycott broadcasters that spread fake news and businesses that advertise on fake news websites. When faced with a decline in business or advertising revenue, large corporations often change their practices. So make your voice heard, and amplify that voice using the same tools that help spread fake news. Only instead of using those tools to perpetuate lies and misinformation, use them to tell the truth and to help strengthen our democracy.

SOURCE NOTES

4   Nolan D. McCaskill, "Trump Accuses Cruz's Father of Helping JFK's Assassin," Politico, May 3, 2016, https://www.politico.com/blogs/2016-gop -primary-live-updates-and-results/2016/05/trump-ted-cruz-father-222730.

4   J. R. Taylor, "Ted Cruz's Father—Caught with JFK Assassin," *National Enquirer*, April 20, 2016, https://www.nationalenquirer.com/celebrity/ted -cruz-scandal-father-jfk-assassination/.

6   "Cannibals Arrested in Florida Claim Eating Human Flesh Cures Diabetes and Depression," WorldTruth.TV, accessed March 12, 2018, http://www .worldtruth.tv/cannibals-arrested-in-florida-claim-eating-human-flesh -cures-diabetes-and-depression/.

6   Hannah Ritchie, "Read All about It: The Biggest Fake News Stories of 2016," *CNBC*, December 30, 2016, https://www.cnbc.com/2016/12/30/read -all-about-it-the-biggest-fake-news-stories-of-2016.html.

6   Shawn Rice, "NYC Muslim Terrorist Donating Thousands to Barack Obama's Campaigns Is Fake News," Business 2 Community, November 4, 2017, https://www.business2community.com/government-politics/nyc -muslim-terrorist-donating-thousands-barack-obamas-campaigns-fake -news-01949068.

7   Emily Stewart, "Study: Conservatives Amplified Russian Trolls 30 Times More Often Than Liberals in 2016," Vox, February 24, 2018, https://www .vox.com/policy-and-politics/2018/2/24/17047880/conservatives-amplified -russian-trolls-more-often-than-liberals.

7   Stewart.

10   Amanda-Mary, "Now It's Official: FDA Announced That Vaccines Are Causing Autism!," Healing Oracle, February 20, 2018, https://www .healingoracle.ch/2018/02/20/now-its-official-fda-announced-that-vaccines -are-causing-autism/.

14   "The Bill of Rights: A Transcription," National Archives, accessed March 13, 2018, https://www.archives.gov/founding-docs/bill-of-rights-transcript.

15   "The Real Story of Fake News," *Merriam-Webster*, accessed May 15, 2018, http://www.merriam-webster.com/words-at-play/the-real-story-of-fake-news.

15   Donald J. Trump, "Donald Trump's News Conference: Full Transcript and Video," *New York Times*, January 11, 2017, https://www.nytimes .com/2017/01/11/us/politics/trump-press-conference-transcript.html.

15   "'Fake News' Is 2017 American Dialect Society Word of the Year," American Dialect Society, January 5, 2018, https://www.americandialect.org/fake-news -is-2017-american-dialect-society-word-of-the-year.

19–20   "SPJ Code of Ethics," Society of Professional Journalists, September 6, 2014, https://www.spj.org/ethicscode.asp.

22 CNN Communications (@CNNPR), Twitter, December 8, 2017, 3:46 p.m., https://twitter.com/cnnpr/status/939234684004962305?lang=en.

29 "Texas Town Quarantined after Family of Five Test Positive for the Ebola Virus," reprinted from the National Report, Myjoyonline.com, October 16, 2014, https://www.myjoyonline.com/world/2014/october-16th/texas-town -quarantined-after-family-of-five-test-positive-for-the-ebola-virus.php.

38 "Drugs Win Drug War," *Onion*, January 10, 1998, available online at https://www.npr.org/assets/news/2013/onion-drugs.pdf.

38 "Study Finds Every Style of Parenting Produces Disturbed, Miserable Adults," *Onion*, October 26, 2011, https://www.theonion.com/study-finds -every-style-of-parenting-produces-disturbed-1819573056.

38 David Edwards, "Fox Nation Readers Confuse *Onion* Article with Real News," Raw Story, November 26, 2010, https://www.rawstory.com/2010/11 /fox-nation-readers-confuse-onion-article-real-news/.

45–46 Terry Collins, "Twitter Says Russian Propaganda More Widespread Than Estimated," CNET, January 19, 2018, https://www.cnet.com/news/twitter -to-notify-users-exposed-to-russian-propaganda/.

46 Eric Johnson, "Full Transcript: Hillary Clinton at Code 2017," Recode, May 31, 2017, https://www.recode.net/2017/5/31/15722218/hillary-clinton -code-conference-transcript-donald-trump-2016-russia-walt-mossberg-kara -swisher.

48 Steven Seidenberg, "Lies and Libel: Fake News Lacks Straightforward Cure," *ABA Journal*, July 2017, http://www.abajournal.com/magazine/article/fake _news_libel_law.

55 Misti Crane, "Reliance on 'Gut Feelings' Linked to Believe in Fake News, Study Finds," Ohio State News, September 18, 2017, https://news.osu.edu /news/2017/09/18/fake-news/.

56 Jay Stanley, "Fixing Fake News," American Civil Liberties Union, December 12, 2016, https://www.aclu.org/blog/free-speech/internet-speech /fixing-fake-news.

57 Brian Resnick, "The Science behind Why Fake News Is So Hard to Wipe Out," Vox, October 31, 2017, https://www.vox.com/science-and-health/2017 /10/5/16410912/illusory-truth-fake-news-las-vegas-google-facebook.

57 Resnick.

65 Cecilia Kang, "Fake News Onslaught Targets Pizzeria as Nest of Child-Trafficking," *New York Times*, November 21, 2016, https://www .nytimes.com/2016/11/21/technology/fact-check-this-pizzeria-is-not-a -child-trafficking-site.html.

65 Faiz Siddiqui and Susan Svrluga, "N.C. Man Told Police He Went to D.C. Pizzeria with Gun to Investigate Conspiracy Theory," *Washington Post*, December 5, 2016, https://www.washingtonpost.com/news/local /wp/2016/12/04/d-c-police-respond-to-report-of-a-man-with-a-gun-at-comet -ping-pong-restaurant/?utm_term=.aafaa5730ced.

65 Christina Zhao, "Man Who Threatened to Kill CNN Employees Over 'Fake News' Arrested," *Newsweek*, January 23, 2018, http://www.newsweek .com/michigan-man-threatens-kill-cnn-employees-brandon-griesemer -crime-787621.

66 Art Swift, "Americans' Trust in Mass Media Sinks to New Low," Gallup, September 14, 2016, news.gallup.com/poll/1600/congress-public.aspx.

68 Thomas Jefferson, "From Thomas Jefferson to James Curie, January 28, 1786," Founders Online, accessed January 15, 2018, https://founders .archives.gov/documents/Jefferson/01-09-02-0209.

70 John McCain, "Mr. President, Stop Attacking the Press," *Washington Post*, January 16, 2018, https://www.washingtonpost.com/opinions/mr -president-stop-attacking-the-press/2018/01/16/9438c0ac-faf0-11e7-a46b -a3614530bd87_story.html?utm_term=.1aaf3082743b.

72 The Bill of Rights: A Transcription," *National Archives*, n.d., www.archives .gov/founding-docs/bill-of-rights-transcript.

73 Benjamin Franklin (as Silence Dogood), "Silence Dogood, No. 8," *New-England Current*, July 9, 1722, https://founders.archives.gov/documents /Franklin/01-01-02-0015.

75 Oliver Wendell Holmes, Schenck v. United States, 249 U.S. 47, 1919.

77 Stanley, "Fake News."

78 Assembly Bill 1104 Chapter 715, "The California Political Cyberfraud Abatement Act," California Legislative Information, October 13, 2017, http://leginfo.legislature.ca.gov/faces/billTextClient.xhtml?bill_id =201720180AB1104.

80 Anthony Faiola and Stephanie Kirchner, "How Do You Stop Fake News? In Germany, with a Law," *Washington Post*, April 5, 2017, https://www .washingtonpost.com/world/europe/how-do-you-stop-fake-news-in -germany-with-a-law/2017/04/05/e6834ad6-1a08-11e7-bcc2-7d1a0973e7b2 _story.html?utm_term=.4c892915679d.

81 Derek Hawkins, "Chobani Sues Alex Jones, Saying He Falsely Linked Company to Child Rape, Tuberculosis," *Washington Post,* April 25, 2017, https://www.washingtonpost.com/news/morning-mix/wp/2017/04/25 /chobani-sues-alex-jones-saying-he-falsely-linked-company-to-child-rape -tuberculosis/?utm_term=.ebaf5b09dcb2.

81 David Montero, "Alex Jones Settles Chobani Lawsuit and Retracts Comments about Twin Falls, Idaho," *Los Angeles Times*, May 17, 2017, http://www.latimes.com/nation/la-na-chobani-alex-jones-20170517 -story.html.

83 "$4 Million and 2 Dead Bodies Found in Democrat Mayor's Storage Unit," USA Mirror News, January 21, 2018, http://usamirrornews.com/4-million -and-2-dead-bodies-found-in-democrat-mayors-storage-unit/.

83 "Morgue Employee Cremated by Mistake While Taking a Nap," World News Daily Report, accessed March 15, 2018, https://worldnewsdailyreport.com /morgue-employee-cremated-by-mistake-while-taking-a-nap/.

83 Aaron Couch and Emmet McDermott, "Donald Trump Campaign Offered Actors $50 to Cheer for Him at Presidential Announcement," *Hollywood Reporter*, June 17, 2015, https://www.hollywoodreporter.com/news/donald -trump-campaign-offered-actors-803161.

84 Daniella Silva, "Elephants Deserve Legal 'Personhood,' New Lawsuit Argues in Connecticut," *NBC News*, November 13, 2017, https://www.nbcnews .com/news/us-news/elephants-deserve-legal-personhood-new-lawsuit-argues -connecticut-n820151.

84 Associated Press, "'Grumpy Cat' Wins $700,000 in Federal Case over Identity," *NBC News*, January 25, 2018, https://www.nbcnews.com/pop -culture/pop-culture-news/grumpy-cat-wins-700-000-federal-case-over -identity-n841076.

84 Olivia Waxman, "Man Shoots at Armadillo but Accidentally Hits His Mother-in-Law," *Time*, April 14, 2015, https://www.time.com/3821026 /armadillo-mother-in-law/.

84 Lindsey Bever, "Man Swept Out to Sea during Sunday Morning Baptism," *Washington Post*, March 31, 2014, https://www.washingtonpost.com/news /morning-mix/wp/2014/03/31/man-swept-out-to-sea-during-sunday-morning -baptism/?utm_term=.1680a0209f1c.

87 Bob Schieffer, "Media Bias?," *CBS News*, February 7, 2005, https://www .cbsnews.com/news/media-bias/.

GLOSSARY

anonymous source: someone interviewed by a reporter who does not want to be named in the resulting news story

artificial intelligence: a machine capable of imitating intelligent human behavior

autocrat: a person who rules with unlimited authority

bias: a preconceived judgment or opinion about a thing, person, group, or idea

bot: a software application that automatically performs repetitive tasks over the internet, such as making Facebook posts or clicking on advertisements to increase website revenue. *Bot* is short for *robot.*

boycott: to refuse to do business with an organization as an expression of disapproval of its practices

clickbait: online content designed to attract attention and encourage visitors to click on a link

confirmation bias: the tendency to believe information that confirms a person's existing beliefs

conspiracy theory: a belief that a secret organization or plot is responsible for an event or situation

democracy: a type of government where people vote for representatives to legislative bodies, such as an assembly, a congress, or a senate

disinformation: false information deliberately spread to influence public opinion or to obscure the truth

echo chamber: an environment in which individuals filter their news consumption—on TV, radio, and the internet—so that they encounter only information and sources that confirm their existing beliefs and opinions

editorial: a newspaper or magazine article, or a segment on a news program, that gives the opinions of the editors, publisher, or other staff member

Fairness Doctrine: a Federal Communications Commission rule (1949 to 1987) that required television and radio stations to promote equal time to both sides of a controversial subject or a political campaign

fake news: news items or social media posts that are mostly or wholly untrue but are designed to look like real news stories. Some leaders use the term to attack legitimate news items and organizations that cast them in an unfavorable light.

freedom of speech: the right to speak out publicly or privately, using any type of media, without interference by the government or private groups. In the United States, the First Amendment protects freedom of speech.

freedom of the press: the right to publish facts, ideas, or opinions without interference from the government or private groups. In the United States, the First Amendment protects the freedom of the press.

illusory truth effect: the tendency to believe information to be true after repeated exposure to it

implicit bias: an automatic and often unconscious prejudice or opinion about a member of a certain racial, ethnic, religious, or other group

journalism: gathering, editing, and disseminating news and information through print publications, television, radio, and online

journalistic integrity: a set of practices and procedures that ensure the accuracy and effectiveness of news reporting

libel: a false written statement that is damaging to a person's reputation or earnings

misinformation: false or misleading information, often deliberately intended to deceive

ombudsman: a staff member who investigates reporting errors and complaints about a news organization

propaganda: biased or misleading information used to promote a particular political cause

pundit: a person who shares expert opinions, usually through mass media

satire: the use of humor to expose or denounce people's vices, stupidity, or actions

search engine optimization: configuring a web page so that it shows up at the top of web search results

slander: a false spoken statement that is damaging to a person's reputation or earnings

tabloid: a newspaper that focuses on sensational stories, such as those dealing with violence, crime, sex, and scandal

SELECTED BIBLIOGRAPHY

Allcott, Hunt, and Matthew Gentzkow. "Social Media and Fake News in the 2016 Election." *Journal of Economic Perspectives* 31, no. 2 (Spring 2017): 211–236. http://web.stanford.edu/~gentzkow/research/fakenews.pdf.

Benedictus, Leo. "Invasion of the Troll Armies: From Russian Trump Supporters to Turkish State Stooges." *Guardian* (US ed.), November 6, 2016. http://www.theguardian.com/media/2016/nov/06/troll-armies-social-media-trump-russian.

Calvert, Clay. "Fake News, Free Speech, and the Third-Person Effect: I'm No Fool, but Others Are." *Wake Forest Law Review*, February 8, 2017. http://www.wakeforestlawreview.com/2017/02/fake-news-free-speech-the-third-person-effect-im-no-fool-but-others-are/.

Collins, Terry, "Twitter Says Russian Propaganda More Widespread Than Estimated." CNET, January 19, 2018. http://www.cnet.com/news/twitter-to-notify-users-exposed-to-russian-propaganda/.

Dewey, Caitlin. "Facebook Fake-News Writer: 'I Think Donald Trump Is in the White House Because of Me.'" *Washington Post*, November 17, 2016. http://www.washingtonpost.com/news/the-intersect/wp/2016/11/17/facebook-fake-news-writer-i-think-donald-trump-is-in-the-white-house-because-of-me/?utm_term=.7ae4f7c4baab.

Gertz, Matt. "New Study: Facebook 'The Most Important Mechanism Facilitating' Fake News." Media Matters, January 2, 2018. http://www.mediamatters.org/blog/2018/01/02/new-study-facebook-most-important-mechanism-facilitating-fake-news/218946.

Gillin, Joshua. "The More Outrageous, the Better: How Clickbait Ads Make Money for Fake News Sites." PolitiFact, October 4, 2017. http://www.politifact.com/punditfact/article/2017/oct/04/more-outrageous-better-how-clickbait-ads-make-mone/.

———. "PolitiFact's Guide to Fake News Websites and What They Peddle." PolitiFact, April 20, 2017. http://www.politifact.com/punditfact/article/2017/apr/20/politifacts-guide-fake-news-websites-and-what-they/.

Nickel, Bradley. "The Dark Side of Display: How 'Fake News' Sites Monetize Their Content." Adbeat. Accessed February 1, 2018. http://www.adbeat.com/blog/fake-news/.

Pearl, Mike. "An Interview with the Former 'Weekly World News' Editor Who Created Bat Boy." Vice, September 30, 2014. http://www.vice.com/en_us/article/8gdkwv/an-interview-with-the-creator-of-bat-boy-987.

———. "The Vegas Shooting Generated Boatloads of Fake News." Vice, October 7, 2017. http://www.vice.com/en_us/article/d3y94z/the-vegas-shooting-generated-boatloads-of-fake-news.

Schulten, Katherine. "Fake News vs. Real News: Determining the Reliability of Sources." *New York Times*, October 2, 2015. https://learning.blogs.nytimes.com/2015/10/02/skills-and-strategies-fake-news-vs-real-news-determining-the-reliability-of-sources/.

Solon, Olivia. "The Future of Fake News: Don't Believe Everything You Read, See or Hear." *Guardian* (US ed.), July 26, 2017. https://www.theguardian.com/technology/2017/jul/26/fake-news-obama-video-trump-face2face-doctored-content.

Sydell, Laura, "We Tracked Down a Fake-News Creator in the Suburbs. Here's What We Learned." *NPR: All Things Considered*, November 23, 2016. https://www.npr.org/sections/alltechconsidered/2016/11/23/503146770/npr-finds-the-head-of-a-covert-fake-news-operation-in-the-suburbs.

Townsend, Tess. "Google Has Banned 200 Publishers since It Passed a New Policy against Fake News." Recode, January 25, 2017. https://www.recode.net/2017/1/25/14375750/google-adsense-advertisers-publishers-fake-news.

Uberti, David. "The Real History of Fake News." *Columbia Journalism Review*, December 15, 2016. https://www.cjr.org/special_report/fake_news_history.php.

FURTHER INFORMATION

BOOKS

Attkisson, Sharyl. *The Smear: How Shady Political Operatives and Fake News Control What You See, What You Think, and How You Vote.* New York: Harper, 2017.

Bartlett, Bruce. *The Truth Matters: A Citizen's Guide to Separating Facts from Lies and Stopping Fake News in Its Tracks.* New York: Ten Speed, 2017.

Hand, Carol. *Everything You Need to Know about Fake News and Propaganda.* New York: Rosen, 2018.

Harris, Duchess. *Freedom of the Press.* Minneapolis: Essential, 2018.

Isikoff, Michael. *Russian Roulette: The Inside Story of Putin's War on America and the Election of Donald Trump.* New York: Twelve, 2018.

Levitin, Daniel J. *Weaponized Lies: How to Think Critically in the Post-Truth Era.* New York: Dutton, 2016.

Levitsky, Steven. *How Democracies Die.* New York: Crown, 2018.

Schwartz, A. Brad. *Broadcast Hysteria: Orson Welles's* War of the Worlds *and the Art of Fake News.* New York: Hill and Wang, 2016.

Shipler, David K. *Freedom of Speech: Mightier Than the Sword.* New York: Vintage, 2016.

Stanley, Jason. *How Propaganda Works.* Princeton, NJ: Princeton University Press, 2016.

Tsipursky, Gleb. *The Truth-Seeker's Handbook: A Science-Based Guide.* Columbus, OH: Intentional Insights, 2017.

WEBSITES

Ethical Journalism Network: Ethics in the News
https://www.ethicaljournalismnetwork.org/resources/publications/ethics-in -the-news
This website examines ethical challenges faced by the media, with a special focus on how fake news impacts traditional journalism.

Harvard Library Research Guides: Fake News, Misinformation, and Propaganda
https://guides.library.harvard.edu/fake
This guide from Harvard University helps media consumers distinguish between fake news and ethical journalism.

Journalism and Media
http://www.journalism.org
The Pew Research Center site offers a variety of articles, statistics, and studies on the news media, social media, media bias, and fake news.